THE MASTER-MISTRESS

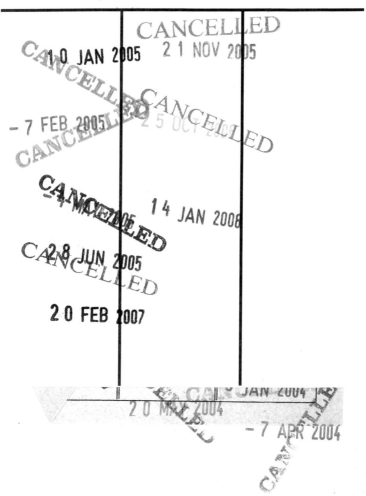

THE
MASTER-MISTRESS

A Study of Shakespeare's Sonnets

by

JAMES WINNY

1968

CHATTO & WINDUS

LONDON

Published by
Chatto & Windus Ltd
40 William IV Street
London W.C.2

★

Clarke, Irwin & Co. Ltd
Toronto

SBN: 7011 1321 9

Printed in Great Britain by
Cox and Wyman Ltd
London, Fakenham and Reading

For my Wife

Contents

CHAPTER ONE

Introduction

THE Sonnets are among the most puzzling of Shakespeare's works. The problem of their significance has been the cause of a controversy longer and more partisan than any of the plays has encouraged, with the single exception of *Hamlet*. These two works have other points in common: in particular a power of inducing in their readers an impression that Shakespeare is personally involved in the feelings of the central figure. The belief that Shakespeare associates himself with Hamlet and speaks his own mind through the Prince will not appeal to a reader who recognises the limits of Hamlet's self-awareness; but the obvious attraction of the idea keeps it alive despite critical attempts to smother it. To simple judgement, the Sonnets offer a closer and more certain contact with Shakespeare's mind and feelings; and once it is suggested that their speaker–himself a poet–is Shakespeare, the notion that the Sonnets are to be read as a journal of their author's private affairs becomes very difficult to discredit. Many poems of the sequence present individual problems of interpretation; but these are overshadowed by the much larger central issue to which Wordsworth returned a simple, comprehensive answer when he declared that in the Sonnets, Shakespeare 'expressed his own feelings in his own person.' His remark helped to promote a critical dispute about the extent of Shakespeare's personal involvement in the story of the Sonnets which continued to inflame opinion throughout the nineteenth century. It remains a subject of controversy; though recently not much has been heard from those who reject the autobiographical theory, and the main field of dispute has shifted. As literary studies are taken over by historians, to whom the stuff of poetry is evidently as factual as pipe-rolls and hearth taxes, arguments over the Sonnets come to centre upon the historical identity of the characters who figure in Shakespeare's story: the Dark Lady, the rival poet, and the young man to whom most of the sonnets are addressed. The aim of this book is to contribute to a better understanding of the Sonnets by exploring a different line of approach, based upon an imaginative interpretation of their meaning.

The possibility that the Sonnets might describe happenings in Shakespeare's private life, and throw light upon his character, seems not to have occurred to any commentator before Malone. When Benson published the pirated edition of 1640, he recommended the poems to his readers for the 'serene, clear and elegantly plain' style which metaphysical wit had driven out of fashion; and did not attempt to make capital out of their interest as biographical material. Probably neither he nor his customers were disposed to regard poetry in this way. Until the Romantic Revival, readers of poetry did not look for disclosures of its author's inmost feelings, and the poet could express ideas through a persona which was not mistaken for his actual self. The later assumption that great poetry must be as immediately personal as *The Prelude* helped to promote a willing belief that the Sonnets have this kind of literal truth. Significantly, the first attempts to fashion a biography of Shakespeare from the Sonnets were made during the heyday of Romanticism, with Wordsworth lending influential support to this critical movement. As the age refashioned the image of Shakespeare bequeathed to it by the editors and commentators of the previous century, it yielded to the pressures of its own mental environment; and saw the Sonnets as the product of an experience as personal and actual as the happenings which formed the subject of much Romantic writing.

The autobiographical theory may have been given its impulse

INTRODUCTION

by Malone, the first of Shakespeare's editors to recognise the possible importance of the Sonnets as a record of the poet's private thoughts and emotions. Although he did not suggest that the sequence could be interpreted throughout in this way, or make any consistent attempt to relate individual poems to events in Shakespeare's life, Malone's notes to his edition of 1790 occasionally assume that the two are linked. Thus he supposes that in Sonnet 111 Shakespeare is lamenting his being 'reduced to the necessity of appearing on the stage, or writing for the theatre': a comment repeated and amplified by later commentators. Malone's remarks on Sonnet 80 reveal the same disposition to treat the poems as literal statements about Shakespeare's private feelings. Although he concedes that Shakespeare had no reason to fear comparison with any other poet of his age, Malone takes the poet at his word when he describes his rival as 'a better spirit'; and explains that Shakespeare was writing when his name was little known, and overshadowed by the fame of Spenser. In general, scholarly respect for evidence seems to restrain him from making any larger claim for the Sonnets; but his remarks on the poet's jealousy in Sonnet 93 typify Malone's readiness to explain Shakespeare in terms of actual life, and not by means of the poem's own terms of reference:

> To attribute to our great poet (to whose amiable manners all his contemporaries bear testimony) the moroseness of a cynic or the depravity of a murderer, would be to form an idea of him contradicted by the whole tenor of his character, and unsupported by any kind of evidence; but to suppose him to have felt a passion which it is said 'most men who ever loved have in some degree experienced,' does not appear to me a very wild or extravagant conjecture.[1]

But a modest conjecture may be as mistaken as an extravagant one, and because Shakespeare was describing a passion familiar to every lover he was not necessarily writing about himself.

3

Yet it would be unfair to expect Malone to recognise the imaginative nature of Shakespeare's work, when critics of an age more respectful towards the creative power of imagination continued to write as though Shakespeare's poetry was drawn from the happenings of everyday life, and that the Sonnets could only represent actual events and persons.

This was the attitude taken up by the German scholar A. W. von Schlegel, who was the first to maintain that the Sonnets were an essentially autobiographical work. Six years after the publication of Malone's edition, von Schlegel drew attention to the special interest which previous editors had overlooked on the Sonnets, observing that without these allusions little or nothing would be known of Shakespeare's personal life. In 1808 he developed this point by remarking that hitherto no commentator had thought of using the Sonnets to piece together a record of Shakespeare's private affairs. He went on:

> These sonnets paint most unequivocally the actual situation and sentiments of the poet; they make us acquainted with the passions of the man; they even contain remarkable confessions of his youthful errors.[2]

Schlegel's opinion, shared and echoed by his brother Friederich in lectures published in 1815, was adopted by several German poets and scholars of note, among them Heine and Ludwig Tieck. In the same year the idea was given further prominence by Wordsworth, whose sweeping declaration in the essay prefixed to his *Poems* has already been quoted. The more famous remark included in one of his own sonnets written twelve years later,

With this key
Shakespeare unlocked his heart,

helped to confirm a belief which by this date had been en-

INTRODUCTION

thusiastically accepted by a number of his fellow-writers, and
as vigorously contested by others.

The controversy produced a sharp and ill-tempered division
between English men of letters. Despite much protest, by the
middle of the nineteenth century the opinion which Wordsworth helped to establish was firmly entrenched, and enjoying
the approval of several Victorian editors who had been won to
its cause. On both sides belief was expressed in absolute and
dogmatic terms, and with no attempt to present a reasoned
case. Furnivall's declaration is typical of this vigorous purpose:

> No one can understand Shakespeare who does not hold that
> his sonnets are autobiographical, and that they explain the
> depths of the soul of the Shakespeare who wrote the plays.[3]

Dowden subscribed to the same article of faith, repeating
Wordsworth's dictum that the Sonnets expressed the poet's
feelings in his own person. Verity in his turn repeated the now
venerable opinion that Shakespeare was 'the real speaker in
every line'[4] of the Sonnets, and asserted that the only rational
course open to the critic was to accept the sequence as a private
confession. Later in the same decade Boas went still further in
support, declaring in *Shakespeare and his Predecessors* that it was

> inconceivable that such intensity of passion as [the Sonnets]
> reveal ... should spring from no solid basis of fact.[5]

Through Raleigh and Bradley, Oxford continued to uphold this argument as the new century opened. Raleigh,
persuaded that the Sonnets were a completely confidential
work 'not intended by Shakespeare for our perusal', followed
Boas in appealing to his readers' intuitive recognition of
poetry based on factual truth. To say that the Sonnets did
not express Shakespeare's feelings in his own person, he wrote,
was

as much as to say that they are not sincere. And every lover of poetry who has once read the Sonnets knows this to be untrue.[6]

Bradley's judgement was more reserved; but he accepted the main contention that the poems represented 'substantially a real story of Shakespeare himself and of certain other persons'; and remarked that if the Sonnets were regarded as 'a free product of mere imagination' certain peculiarities in the story would become unaccountable.[7] For this suggestion Bradley was probably indebted to the American critic H. C. Beeching, who five years earlier had objected that so talented a writer *to no story* would not deliberately have devised so incoherent a story. This point was repeated by other commentators, none of whom can have reflected that disjointed narrative form is not a reliable guide to the truthfulness of a story. In the twenties, J. Middleton Murry dismissed all doubt by affirming that it was 'impossible for anyone but a briefed advocate' to maintain that the Sonnets are not substantially 'the record of the poet's own disaster in love.'[8] The most eminent Shakespearian scholar of the period, E. K. Chambers, seemed at first to hesitate over the issue which others had determined so positively; though when he outlined *in accordance with Schiller* the subject-matter of the Sonnets in his *Facts and Problems* he did not treat the figures and happenings of the story as fictional. In *Shakespearean Gleanings,* published fourteen years later, he made his views a little clearer by conceding that the order of the Sonnets is 'an autobiographical one, following the ups and downs of an emotional relationship.'[9] If Chambers' private convictions were any stronger than these comments suggested, he concealed them more successfully than did C. S. Lewis in his *English Literature of the Sixteenth Century.* Although he tries to assume a neutral position towards the controversy, when Lewis speaks of the emotional detachment of the Sonnets he betrays his belief that Shakespeare is writing of himself. 'He left it to his created persons,' Lewis remarks, his Lears and Othellos, to pour out raw experience, scalding hot. In his own person he does not do so.[10]

Among these 'created persons' the speaker of the Sonnets is plainly not to be included. The most recent editor of the Sonnets, J. Dover Wilson, embraces the autobiographical theory with a fervour that recalls its Victorian adherents; neither acknowledging how great a body of dissenting opinion exists nor offering to adjudicate between the two arguments. Taking the literal truth of the Sonnets as self-evident, he invites his readers to share his belief in a Friend who contributed sonnets to the sequence, and in a Dark Lady who treacherously sold Shakespeare's manuscript to the printer.[11]

The motives which induced so many critics to accept the Sonnets as literally true despite a complete lack of independent evidence lies outside the scope of this survey. It seems clear that the belief was impelled by a strong wish that it should be true, and that the energy of the assertion was a measure of this desire rather than of any rational conviction. The obvious appeal of the autobiographical theory was that it brought Shakespeare into immediate personal range, as a great and noble figure with whom the delighted reader could feel himself intimately associated. The kind of satisfaction which rewarded those who accepted the Sonnets as a private document is shown by the awed reverence of an American critic, writing in 1864:

> We seem to stand by the door of the confessional, and listen to the most secret secrets in the heart of Shakespeare. These mysteries are veiled in a language so wonderfully delicate that it at once tells all and tells nothing.[12]

In fact, the language of the Sonnets sometimes falls well short of delicacy, and the poet's allusions to his relationship are occasionally less ambigious than those who idealise Shakespeare might wish. Perhaps the most powerful motive for rejecting the autobiographical theory sprang from this fact. In itself, the attraction of being admitted to Shakespeare's confessional might have been irresistible; but eavesdroppers must be prepared to hear some unpalatable secrets, and not all the Sonnets' disclosures were compatible with moral integrity in their author. Dyce might assure his readers that nothing could be inferred from the Sonnets about Shakespeare's moral character; but when he tries to crush the imputation that the married poet 'was by no means remarkable for purity of morals', he writes like a man holding a nagging suspicion at bay. His comment understates the gravity of the charge which could be brought against Shakespeare. If the Sonnets had the literal truth claimed for them, it would be difficult to resist the inference that Shakespeare was a homosexual and an adulterer, who had been involved in a particularly shameful liaison with a woman of scandalous reputation. Readers who heard Shakespeare speaking in every word of the Sonnets seem to have been too enraptured by the experience to recognise the moral implications of the attachments which they describe. On the other side the challenge of these disturbing revelations was more honestly met, and the hatefulness of what they seemed to imply caused the auto-biographical theory to be treated as an outrageous and indefensible slander. A society whose public standards of morality were so inflexible and ungenerous found the task of reconciling Shakespeare's human and poetic authority with sexual laxity and perversion impossibly taxing, and compelled its critics to choose between burking the issue of Shakespeare's private behaviour and denying that the Sonnets had any bearing on actual affairs. The self-degradation which the poems admitted, one commentator wrote, was 'sufficient to prove that Shakespeare spoke not for himself.'[13] His remark characterises a widely shared determination to protect an ideal conception of the poet by outlawing in advance any disclosure that might bring his name into discredit.

INTRODUCTION

It may have been some other motive which persuaded Campbell to throw his editorial weight against Wordsworth in 1838, but many later critics made no secret of their anxiety to protect Shakespeare's reputation by denying that the Sonnets told a true story. Campbell's firm conviction that the Sonnets threw no light upon the poet's personal history was echoed by Collier, who had already declared his 'extremely probable' belief that some of the Sonnets had been written

> for other people, who could not write for themselves, and who wished to make a favourable impression.[14]

Collier was later to abandon this fanciful hypothesis, which was adopted by Dyce as a convenient means of refuting any assumption that the Dark Lady sonnets represented a shameful passage in Shakespeare's private affairs. For Dyce it was unthinkable that poems admitting sexual misconduct could have been written in Shakespeare's own person. By borrowing Collier's idea he was able to clear the poet of suspicion, arguing that since most of the Sonnets 'appear to have been written under an assumed character',[15] nothing could be inferred from them about the poet's private behaviour. Once committed to hypotheses, Dyce evidently found it difficult to restrain his ingenuity. Admitting later in his preface that a few sonnets might have some bearing upon Shakespeare's actual experience, he reaffirmed that elsewhere Shakespeare adopts a persona, and offered the novel suggestion that this device had been proposed by the poet's friends. The younger Hazlitt, who was prepared to regard the story of the Sonnets as 'entirely imaginary', followed Dyce in supposing that its darker episodes must have been provided by some other mind. 'The fanciful hint of a friend,' he wrote,

> may have originated the sonnets which, as applied to any conceivable state of facts, appear so inexplicable.[16]

B

9

Halliwell-Phillipps too found himself unable to accept a reading of the Sonnets which brought Shakespeare into disrepute; but he also exposed a weakness of the autobiographical theory by observing that, if it were true, Shakespeare had revealed his vicious habit of life not merely to a later age but to the circle of friends who saw his poems in manuscript. 'If the personal theory is accepted,' he pointed out,

> we must concede the possibility of our national dramatist gratuitously confessing his own sins and revealing those of others, proclaiming his disgrace and avowing his repentance, in poetic circulars distributed by the delinquent himself amongst his own intimate friends.[17]

This objection presented a stronger argument of probability against the literalists' case than any of its advocates had put forward; but a single probability could not settle a dispute whose contestants were so deeply committed to their beliefs. To declare that Shakespeare cannot have been a sycophant, a flatterer, a breaker of marriage vows, a whining and inconstant person,[18] was to beg the question: we do not know what sort of man he was. Symonds might warn critics of the Sonnets not to construct 'a biographical romance out of elements so slender' until they had access to reliable information from other sources,[19] but neither side was primarily interested in establishing the truth in a disinterested and scholarly fashion. To enjoy an illusion of intimate association with Shakespeare, or to repudiate the most damaging of slanders on his personal character, commentators were ready to employ the crudest forms of argument and to resort to bare, defiant statements of faith which appealed only to prejudice. So Crosland, in *The English Sonnet*, answered Wordsworth in the idiom of the schoolroom by announcing categorically that Shakespeare 'did NOT unlock his heart in the Sonnets'; and developed his point in a series of dogmatic and entirely unsupported assumptions:

We contend further that he had no 'fair male friend' and no 'dark naughty woman-love' such as the Sonnets shadow-forth ... 'The story of the Sonnets', such as it is, was evolved fortuitously out of the writing and sequence of the pieces, and the sonnets were not written out of a story, personal or impersonal.[20]

By the date of Crosland's book the autobiographical theory had been shaken by studies in the history and development of the sonnet, which showed that many of Shakespeare's poems borrow from a stock of traditional ideas and attitudes common to Renaissance sonnet-writers. Against the discovery that much of Shakespeare's material was not original, adherents of the theory could reply that emotions are not necessarily insincere or fictional because they make use of traditional forms of complaint, and that Shakespeare's borrowings showed him reanimating sonnet form rather than adapting himself to an inflexible tradition. But the knowledge that the Sonnets were not entirely original in conception checked the extremist view that Shakespeare is the real speaker in every line, and strengthened those who already denied it on other grounds. This shift of critical attitude had its beginnings in Lee's study of the Elizabethan sonnet, published in 1904. Finding 'adapted or imitated conceits scattered over the whole of Shakespeare's collection', and affirming that imitation and true feeling could never go hand in hand, Lee gave his opinion that it was not possible to treat the Sonnets as personal confession. Nearly twenty years later, in his *Sketch of Recent Shakespearean Investigation* C. H. Herford echoed this judgement, observing that

> the derivative character of a vast majority of the sonnets does much ... to invalidate whatever claim they make (and many make no such claim) to be outpourings of sincere emotion, to be taken at their face value.[21]

In the following year Tucker issued a carefully worded caveat

against supposing that all the poems contributed to a true story.
It was mistaken, he said,

> either to treat every piece alike as being concerned with one
> and the same object of affection, or to regard the whole series
> as being an equally spontaneous and emotionally consistent
> record of the poet's relations with that object.[22]

The passage shows Tucker trying to sidestep the crucial issue by
implying that the Sonnets both are and are not autobiographical.
Such hedging of the question was not new. From the beginning
of the controversy, well-meaning attempts had been made to
settle the dispute through an obvious form of compromise.
Thus in 1836 an unidentified contributor to *The Westminster
Review* refused to accept Schlegel's opinion that the Sonnets
were literally true, but was prepared to admit that they might
be 'partly autobiographical'; evidently consulting only his
private feelings about the limits of their truth. The poems might
afford 'useful hints and traces' of Shakespeare's character, but
they were 'not to be relied on for the incidents of the life'.[23] In
his edition of 1841, Knight inclined towards the autobiographical view but recoiled almost visibly from the full consequences of this belief. The Sonnets were personal in their
form, he admitted, but

> it is not therefore to be assumed that they are *all* personal in
> their relation to the author.[24]

His point was repeated a little later in Chambers's *Cyclopaedia,*
whose writer sought to distinguish between poems which
expressed Shakespeare's true feelings and others 'written in a
feigned character.'[25] Lee proposed a similar compromise as a
means of resolving the deadlock between the two main points
of view. Although ready to regard most of the sonnets as
'merely literary meditations',[26] Lee made it clear that the

Friend, the rival poet and Mr W. H. were to be considered as actual persons whom it might be possible to identify. Bradley too was prepared to adopt a position midway between the contestants. Some of the poems, he thought, might be 'mere exercises of art'; but he declined to treat the whole sequence as fictional.[27] Like him, E. B. Reed attempted to express his disagreement with the dogmatic assumption made by Wordsworth, but without dissociating himself from it entirely. Shakespeare may not have unlocked his heart in the Sonnets, Reed proposed pleasantly, 'but surely at times he left the door ajar.'[28] Robertson, in *Shakespeare and Chapman*, 1917, acknowledged that a large number of the poems might be autobiographical; but argued that others must be read as poems written 'on behalf of, or at the instance of, various personages'[29] whom Robertson does not identify, but who were perhaps known to Collier and others in the previous century. In a more recent study of the Sonnets, Young is prepared to adopt either view of their nature impartially. The poems certainly tell a story, he remarks, and this remains the same whether it is true or simply a romantic invention.[30]

Such attempts to evade the main issue of Shakespeare's personal involvement in all the Sonnets were censured by Lee in the original version of the essay on the poet which he contributed to the *Dictionary of National Biography* in 1897. Those who tried to pass off the Sonnets as literary exercises, Lee declared, were motivated by reluctance to acknowledge facts which might injure Shakespeare's moral reputation. As though himself yielding to the same anxiety, he then cancelled this passage of his biography; but the attack was renewed in 1900 by the French critic Fernand Henry, who remarked that only English prudery and cant could be troubled by what the Sonnets disclosed. Lee's recantation incurred the scorn of Louis Gillet, who saw no purpose in trying to suppress these revelations, even though the truth happened to be horrible and atrocious. 'Such frankness is painful,' he admitted, 'but if this drama is to be conjured away, let us give up all idea of understanding Shakespeare.'[31] With the spread of more permissive moral standards the issue has lost most of its urgency; and it may be for this reason that critical dispute now centres upon different versions of the autobiographical theory, and that the simple conflict between literal and figurative readings of the Sonnets has lapsed. At least one recent editor, however, has been glad of an authoritative assurance that Shakespeare is clear of one unpleasant suspicion; and there may be others who have felt relieved by C. S. Lewis in his summing-up. 'This does not seem to be the poetry of full-blown pederasty.'

To a modern student of the controversy it must seem curious that neither side suggested that the Sonnets were to be read as a work of imaginative creation. Either they were literally true or they were fictional, by which opposers of the autobiographical theory seem to have meant that their story and characters were simply invented, for a purpose which was left unexplained. If there was no literal truth in the odd story of the Sonnets, what had Shakespeare intended it to represent? In the excitement of controversy this question was overlooked: the major issue in dispute was whether or not the Sonnets constituted a private confession. To the extent that poetry is to be judged by standards of imaginative truth, this issue made itself irrelevant by confusing the nature of poetry with the terms of actual existence. To argue whether or not the events and persons described in the Sonnets had actually occurred or existed was as much beside the point as to raise similar questions about Rosalind or King Lear: they did and do exist in those terms in which the poet has created them, and not otherwise. From time to time isolated critics have tried to bring this point into the controversy over the Sonnets. In 1855 Robert Bell suggested that the main dispute might not be to the purpose, observing that all poetry is autobiographical. He was not prepared to admit that a poem might be entirely independent of the poet's everyday experience; but, he wrote,

> the particle of actual life out of which verse is wrought may be, and almost always is, wholly incommensurate to the emotion depicted, and remote from the forms into which it is ultimately shaped.[32]

Although he did not allow that the germ of a poem might be offered to the poet by his imaginative experience, Bell might have initiated a more discerning appreciation of what the Sonnets represent; but his comments seem to have passed unnoticed. In 1874 von Friesen followed Bell's lead by describing the Sonnets as the poetic residue of personal experiences, either real or imagined: a thoughtful view which holds autobiography at a distance, and conceded that whatever the poet draws from actual life is refashioned in the imagination before it becomes poetry. In electing to see the Sonnets as 'the events of actuality transmuted by imagination',[33] von Friesen implied that they were to some extent 'true', though perhaps not easily recognisable as such. He and Bell might have agreed that the Sonnets were related to actuality in much the same way as *Resolution and Independence* was related to Wordsworth's actual meeting with the leech-gatherer towards evening on the road to Keswick; and that they were unlike *Kubla Khan*, whose story reflected nothing that happened to Coleridge in the world of material events. This view of the Sonnets was supported by Hadow in 1907. There was a strong likelihood, he suggested, that the poems were written

> when a story suggesting that which they narrate actually occurred, and that Shakespeare used it with the same imaginative latitude with which he rewrote the history of King Lear.[34]

But Hadow's phrase 'imaginative latitude' does not in fact admit that the creative force of imagination was brought into play. His suggestion implies only that Shakespeare varied the circumstances of an actual experience, not that the Sonnets grew out of a prolonged imaginative reflection. Hadow's final judgement, that the possibility of such events having happened was unthinkable, shows him recoiling from the prospect which had driven other critics to challenge the autobiographical theory with blunter arguments. Six years later, in *The Facts about Shakespeare,* Neilson and Thorndike reminded their readers that Shakespeare's poetry did not depend upon actual experience for its stimulus. Declaring plainly that the Sonnets afforded no knowledge of his personal life, they remarked that it was

> hardly necessary to urge that Shakespeare was capable of profound and passionate utterance under the impulse of imagination alone.[35]

In fact, their reminder was badly needed.

Meanwhile in Germany a similar tendency to reject the conception of poetry as a literal record of experience showed itself in a growing inclination to regard the Sonnets as the work of a poet, not of a diarist. At the height of the 1914–18 war Heinrich Mutschmann contributed to this better appreciation of Shakespeare by drawing an analogy with Goethe,

> whose poems, according to his own statement, are 'fragments of a great confession,' and who yet, with the most ravishing powers of conviction, describes lyrical situations which have no basis in actual, or rather, physical experience.

He went on to make what was then a novel suggestion, that the Sonnets should not be considered in isolation from the rest of Shakespeare's work, to which they were closely related by common imaginative interests:

> I do not believe that one can separate the sonnets from the narrative poems and these from the plays. The same questions,

16

the same conflicts, the same problems, recur in all three categories.[36]

War prevented Mutschmann's ideas attracting the wider attention which they deserved; though as he himself acknowledged, most scholars of Shakespeare were too stubbornly fixed in their beliefs to be affected by any critical reappraisal of the Sonnets. For those still open to persuasion, John Bailey observed simply that something more than familiarity with Elizabethan literary traditions should warn us against looking for a life of Shakespeare in the Sonnets:

> the nature of poetry itself. Poetry is imagination, not fact.[37]

But the belief persists that the Sonnets tell a true story, and that imagination supplied nothing but the splendid terms in which their events are described. Dover Wilson, whose faith in the literal truth of the story carries him so far as supposing that Sonnet 20 'might have been occasioned by a bathe in the Thames',[38] writes as though the autobiographical theory were completely tenable and the meaning of the Sonnets self-evident, in their account of Shakespeare's actual relationship with a no less actual and identifiable friend.

Against such a literal reading of the Sonnets it may be enough to object that poetry does not share the nature of historical documents. At its best, poetry does not describe happenings at all: it causes them to occur within the reader's mind. It is in this sense that poetry is creative. When Shakespeare brings about such an imaginative event we have no reason to suppose that the poem duplicates, in its way, some physical experience which he had recently undergone. The most we can assume is that the poem represents the nature of the particular imaginative experience which prompted him to write. By following this thread we may hope to reach an understanding of the imaginative happening which the poem recreates; but by regarding the poem as an account of events whose nature is not imaginative but historical we transfer attention from the poet's intensely personal experience to the world of common fact, and lose contact with the poem and its meaning. The reader of the Sonnets who prefers to pursue the cryptic figure of Mr W. H. through the by-ways of Elizabethan literary and social history may become minutely familiar with the lives and characters of several likely associates of Shakespeare; but he will not be moving towards an understanding of the Sonnets as poetry.

Even without this fundamental objection to a literal interpretation of the Sonnets, the theory is open to serious doubts on the grounds of its improbability. That the story is disjointed and contradictory, and that it brings Shakespeare's moral character into hazard, proves nothing either way. Where the theory loses all likelihood, as Halliwell-Phillipps pointed out, is in requiring its supporters to believe that Shakespeare, having formed an equivocally close liaison with a young nobleman, wrote and circulated poems describing the course of their relationship, revealing that this idol of society was dissolute, hypocritical and disloyal; apparently without arousing resentment. Defenders of the theory may suggest that those 'sugred sonnets' which Shakespeare had allowed to circulate among his private friends by 1598 were the innocuous poems of the sequence; that the two possibly defamatory sonnets included in *The Passionate Pilgrim* were published without Shakespeare's consent; and that the 1609 Quarto owed its appearance to acts of piracy and betrayal, which exposed a highly confidential work to the common reader. The burden of proof rests with them. They must also explain why the disclosure of Shakespeare's evidently compromising relationship with so well-known a figure as the Sonnets describe aroused no comment at the time, and – although amply supported by the poems themselves – gave rise to no scandal when they were published. There may have been a grand conspiracy of silence involving stationers, rival poets, gossip-mongers and contemporary historians and journalists; but it is easier to believe that the Sonnets do not allude to actual persons and events. They may have been published without his consent or approval; but it is clear from textual confusion in the plays that Shakespeare took little interest in seeing his work printed. If the 1609 Quarto was unauthorised, there are no grounds for supposing that Shakespeare wished the Sonnets to remain unpublished. Had he wished them to keep their secret, he would not have put them into limited circulation among his friends. The puzzle of what motive should have induced Shakespeare to darken his gentle reputation by publicly confessing himself waits to be answered by those who maintain the autobiographical theory. It may be possible to envisage a poet ready to compromise his good name for the pleasure of making known his intimate friendship with a young nobleman; though such a purpose is incompatible with the self-abnegating love which the poet professes towards the friend. It is more difficult to imagine a married man openly admitting his association with a mistress; the more so when the lady is ill-favoured as well as inconstant, and when the man feels exasperation and self contempt both in and out of her company. Sexual humiliation is an indignity which most lovers prefer to conceal, especially from the wives to whom they are being faithless.

Probability is not a sure guide to truth; but against the unlikelihoods which the literal interpretation involves only a very hardy or a very stubborn critic would persist. Lacking other evidence, the story itself must be made to confirm the belief which the autobiographical theory takes as its point of departure. But the story can be read variously by different readers, and without always leaving the impression of a true report in Shakespeare's own words. A few sonnets may glance allusively at current events. Whether the 'mortal moon' of Sonnet 107 refers to an enduring Queen or to a ruined Armada—

even here, with no apparent need to pick his words diplomatically, the poet speaks indefinitely–Shakespeare is making some topical occurrence serve his larger purpose. To this limited extent he may occasionally be present as commentator, though without revealing more of himself than a familiarity with public affairs. There is little here, or elsewhere in the sequence, to suggest that Shakespeare intends to make a public investigation of his personal being; and still less to support the belief that the story follows the course of an actual relationship. What might be regarded as a narrative thread running through the Sonnets is disconnected and erratic. If there is a story, it develops irregularly; usually in the form of instalments each consisting of a few sonnets on a common or partly shared theme–absence, sleeplessness, rivalry, estrangement, neglect– and reaching no clear dénouement. There are too many gaps in the account, too many unexplained consequences, and too much variation of circumstance for it to seem likely that Shakespeare was transcribing from life. Where the term 'story' suggests purposeful narrative growth, the sequence develops like a man leaping from stone to stone across a stream, with no distinct idea where he will reach the farther bank.

The disjointed form of this tenuous narrative and its random development have been seen as proving that the Sonnets do not tell a fictional story. A writer as inventive as Shakespeare, the literalists have maintained, would have devised a more coherent and plausible mock-autobiography. They might have added that if it had been his purpose to write a narrative poem, a sonnet-sequence was a curious medium to have chosen. But if the course of experience followed by the Sonnets is not fictional but imaginative, this argument falls to the ground. In its erratic growth and inconsistency of detail the story is certainly unlike the kind of formal narrative which might have been expected of a poet intent upon fiction; but these very features help to identify the Sonnets as an imaginative work, in which the poet is searching deeply, and often without certainty, into the working of his creative consciousness. Mutschmann's remark about the way the same questions, conflicts and problems recur throughout Shakespeare's writing, whether drama or poems, deserves to be remembered. The dominant ideas and interests of the Sonnets are not peculiar to them, but shared with the two narrative poems and with some of the plays. This likeness extends to many of the situations which the poet encounters in the sequence; and it includes the form of uneasy, unresolved relationship which both joins the poet with his friend and obstructs their union. Such imaginative similarities make it difficult to regard the Sonnets as a body of writing entirely separate from the rest of Shakespeare's work; and urge us to recognise them as a half-private adjunct of his main creative activity, in which some of the ideas which most preoccupy him are worked over intensively, within the brief limits of a single personal relationship.

Perhaps we should see this activity as intermittent, producing a group of sonnets on a common theme and falling silent again. The simple notion of a varying friendship provides a rudimentary narrative thread to which the Sonnets are loosely attached; but Shakespeare's interest is concentrated upon the individual situation which each sonnet explores, and not upon the plot which barely holds them together. Breaks in the story, and inconsistency over matters of detail, would follow naturally if the poems were written in groups at irregular intervals, as their ideas developed. If the whole sequence was produced over a period of five years, which is probably a conservative estimate, the Shakespeare who completed the Sonnets had moved imaginatively a long way from his starting-point. We should expect this change to be reflected in the poems; in their increased maturity and self-awareness, and also in mismatching between different episodes of the story. When Shakespeare returned to his sonnet-sequence after an interval occupied by dramatic writing, he may have found it impossible to take up the story of the poet's unstable friendship at the point where his imagination had left it, or to fit his now modified ideas into the same narrative outline.

To argue that the Sonnets are neither autobiographical nor fictional, and that in another sense they are both these things, will seem perverse only if we have not tried to grasp the nature of imaginative experience. When Robert Bell observed that all poetry is autobiographical he was recognising that, whatever his subject, the poet cannot avoid describing and revealing himself. The world he creates is the world of his own consciousness: its horrors and delights are his own. Whether he intends it or not, he is providing insight into the private experience which includes not just the happenings of actual life, but the half-world of his unconscious mind, his dreams and their symbolic creatures. What may seem fictional is the reality of his subjective being, and the autobiography of the self whose field of experience extends far beyond the limits of waking actuality. The Sonnets may be unconnected with Shakespeare's experience within this actual world, yet autobiographical in that they represent happenings inside the much more extensive private world which is the field of his creative consciousness. If the events which they appear to describe did not actually take place, something corresponding to those events did happen within this imaginative field, whose nature and significance have not yet been explained. Those Victorian critics who recognise the cryptic character of the Sonnets generally supposed that Shakespeare was speaking guardedly for diplomatic reasons, and that the poems would give up their secrets when historical fact could be brought to bear upon problems of human identity. Belief that the Sonnets were a chapter of autobiography 'remaining in cypher till criticism finds the key',[39] remains a spur to the kind of inquiry which seeks to elucidate poetry through historical research. According to Boulenger's count, by 1919 about seventy such keys had been discovered. Their number still increases; but against the hope that the Sonnets would eventually be explained with the help of historical evidence the most influential critic of his age remarked in 1927:

> This autobiography is written by a foreign man in a foreign tongue, which can never be translated.[40]

We are not obliged to share Eliot's certainty that the mystery is insoluble. We have his own assurance that the whole of Shakespeare's work 'is *one* poem . . . united by one significant, consistent, and developing personality';[41] and if this is true, the disclosure of personality in the Sonnets forms only part of the much fuller revelation which the plays and poems together afford. What we learn of Shakespeare from his dramatic work is of help in reading the chapter of imaginative autobiography that is written into the Sonnets. Those figures and situations of the Sonnets which recur in the plays, modified but not essentially changed, tell us something about the imaginative pressures which have shaped them. We begin to identify the imaginative preoccupations which Shakespeare never entirely shakes off; and to piece together an outline of the intensely personal experience which the poet has represented in his curious story, whose emotions have been happily described as refusing to fit into our pigeon-holes. We also realise more clearly how little Shakespeare's work tells us about the man, whose actual experience was so far overshadowed by the happenings of his imaginative life. That he had noble friends, that William Herbert was one of them, and that some sonnets are addressed to a patron, are all possible and irrelevant to the meaning of the sequence. A great poet does not write to convey private sentiments to a friend, but to give realised form to his imaginative experience. Shakespeare achieved this purpose most completely in his plays. The Sonnets realise a limited though perhaps crucial part of that experience. Possibly they are, as so many readers have felt, more directly associated with the personality of Shakespeare than any other of his works. But when we speak of Shakespeare's 'personality' we refer to the being described by the continuous poem of his whole *oeuvre*, not to the man whose public face stares uncommunicatively from the Droeshout portrait. What we learn of Shakespeare from the Sonnets throws no light upon his domestic affairs, any more than do the plays. Rather—like them, but without their direct enacting of the poet's imaginative concerns—the Sonnets disclose allusively the form of the interior life that is both Shakespeare's constant subject and the source of his impulse to create.

NOTES

1 Edmond Malone, *The Plays and Poems of William Shakespeare,* London 1790; x.268.

2 A. W. von Schlegel, *A Course of Lectures,* tr. Black and Morrison; London 1846, p. 352.

3 F. J. Furnivall, *The Leopold Shakespeare;* London 1877, p. lxvi.

4 A. W. Verity, *Pitt Press Shakespeare,* Cambridge 1890–1905; p. 399 f.

5 F. S. Boas, *Shakespeare and his Predecessors;* Oxford 1896, p. 115.

6 Walter Raleigh, *Shakespeare;* Oxford 1907, pp. 87 f.

7 A. C. Bradley, *Oxford Lectures;* London 1909, p. 330.

8 J. M. Murry, *Countries of the Mind* Series 1; London 1922, p. 11.

9 E. K. Chambers, *Shakespearean Gleanings;* London 1944, p. 120.

10 C. S. Lewis, *English Literature in the Sixteenth Century;* Oxford 1954, p. 508.

11 J. D. Wilson, *The Sonnets;* Cambridge 1966; pp. xl–xli.

12 J. F. Clarke, *Memorial and Biographical Sketches;* New York 1878, p. 315.

13 R. G. White, *Shakespeare's Scholar;* New York 1854, p. 474.

14 J. P. Collier, *History of English Dramatic Poetry;* London 1831, i.330.

15 Alexander Dyce, *The Poems of Shakespeare;* London 1832, pp. xlf–xif.

16 William Hazlitt, *Supplementary Works of Shakespeare;* London 1852, p. 454.

17 J. O. Halliwell-Phillipps, *The Works of Shakespeare;* London 1853–65, xvi. 369.

18 Ebenezer Forsyth, *Shakespeare;* Edinburgh 1867, p. 22.

19 J. A. Symonds, *Essays Speculative;* London 1890, i. 118.

20 T. W. H. Crosland, *The English Sonnet;* London 1917, pp. 211–213.

21 C. H. Herford, *A Sketch of recent Shakespearean Investigations;* London 1923, p. 56.

22 T. G. Tucker, *The Sonnets of Shakespeare;* London 1924, p. xxxvi.

23 *The London and Westminster Review,* XXVI; London 1836, p.18.

24 Charles Knight, *The Works of Shakespeare;* London 1846, xii. 192.

25 Robert Chambers, *Cyclopaedia of English Literature;* Edinburgh 1844, i. 105.

26 Sidney Lee, *Life of Shakespeare;* London 1898, p. 152.

27 A. C. Bradley, *op. cit.,* p. 330.

28 E. B. Reed, *Shakespeare's Sonnets;* New Haven 1923, p. 95.

29 J. M. Robertson, *Shakespeare and Chapman;* London 1917, p. 12.

30 M. McC. Young, *The Sonnets of Shakespeare;* Madison 1936, p. 2.

31 Louis Gillet, *Shakespeare;* London 1931, p. 144.

32 Robert Bell, *The Poems of Shakespeare;* London 1855, p. 152.

33 Hermann von Friesen, *Shakespeare-Studien* 1874, p. 338.

34 W. H. Hadow, *Shakespeare's Sonnets;* London 1907, p. x.

35 W. A. Neilson and A. H. Thorndike, *The Facts about Shakespeare;* New York 1913, p. 88.

36 Heinrich Mutschmann, *Beiblatt* XXVII, 1916, p. 168.

37 John Bailey, *Shakespeare;* London 1929, pp. 59 f.

38 J. Dover Wilson, *ed. cit.,* p. 117.

39 R. A. Willmott, *Journal of Summer Time,* 1849, p. 19.

40 T. S. Eliot, *Nation and Athenaeum* XL; London 1927, p. 666.

41 T. S. Eliot, *Selected Essays,* London 1932, p. 203.

CHAPTER TWO
The Story

THE story of the Sonnets is at best tenuous. It has a central topic in the poet's relationship with the 'lovely boy' who is last addressed on Sonnet 126, before attention shifts to the Dark Lady; but not all the poems in the sequence 1–126 are connected with this relationship. Several represent private reflections in which no second person is involved. Over the whole sequence of a hundred and fifty-four sonnets, although most are addressed to the friend or the mistress, some of the most powerful of them are impersonal pronouncements, which if relevant to the story make no allusion to any of its three main characters. Sonnet 94, 'Those that have power to hurt', and Sonnet 129, 'The expense of spirit', figure in this small but important group of poems which lie outside the story. Others, of which Sonnet 26 is an example, are not certainly addressed to the same noble patron as the poems of the main sequence hint at. Nothing in the more famous Sonnet 116, 'Let me not to the marriage', obliges us to suppose that the poet is still addressing the friend: as in the last of the poems on Time, Sonnet 123, he seems to be declaring his position to himself without looking towards an audience. Critics who have made these and other detached sonnets part of the story have done so without encouragement from the poet. Even to see a story in the sequence as a whole requires something of an act of faith. There is certainly no suggestion of narrative purpose in the group of twelve or more sonnets which opens the series, where the poet demonstrates his wit in a set of variations on the theme of increase.

Of the many sonnets addressed directly to the friend, few make any attempt to develop a story-line by describing the background of the situation on which they comment, or by relating their narrative fragment to a larger scheme of happenings. Sonnet 104 provides the tantalising scrap of information that the poet first met the friend three years earlier, but nothing in the sequence supplements this fact. Nothing suggests where the poet was going when he rode away from the friend in Sonnet 50, or what business prompted his absence; and although commentators have been quick to remedy this omission and even to propose dates for the journey, the indefiniteness of the poet's allusion, and the lack of narrative link with other similarly isolated incidents, typify the incoherence of the story. If we are to be fair to Shakespeare, we shall not suggest that he is attempting to present a work whose kind is primarily narrative. The Sonnets are strung together in a way which suggests very little concern with whatever story they might be made to tell; and even if it is argued that Thorpe disturbed their proper order, the kind of rearrangement usually proposed merely groups together all the sonnets bearing on common themes. Such groups, dealing with absence, estrangement or poetic rivalry, already exist in the sequence; providing the fixed points between which the autobiographical theorists draw the story-line of the Sonnets. If the resulting story is fragmentary and implausible, we cannot very well complain that Shakespeare is no narrative poet. The form of the sequence suggests a quite different intention.

Shakespeare's purpose in the Sonnets is implicit in the opening group of poems on marriage and increase, and in the two final poems of the sequence. The latter, Sonnets 153 and 154, are generally looked upon as an appendix not connected with the story, which Shakespeare or the printer added simply to enlarge the collection. Both tell a fanciful story about the origins of a medicinal spring, brought into being when a nymph extinguished Cupid's torch in a well, which 'took heat perpetual' from this fire. The second version tells a more leisurely

tale, taking nine lines to relate the matter which Sonnet 153
fits into four, and the couplets draw different conclusions; but
the matter of the two poems is effectively the same. Malone
supposed that Shakespeare could not have intended both to be
published and that he had not decided which version he
preferred. This may be true; but the possibilities are less
interesting than the fact that on one occasion at least Shakespeare wrote two versions of the same sonnet, as though
experimenting with his presentation of ideas. The group of
marriage-sonnets which opens the sequence limits its field of
ideas almost as severely as this linked pair. The poet varies the
form of his argument slightly from poem to poem, but without
losing contact with the basic ideas which he continues to explore. The first ten of these sonnets are held together by a
community of thought which imposes a strict economy of
idea upon the poet's repeated arguments in favour of marriage;
and the subject is not abandoned until its potentialities have
been squeezed dry. Thus similes involving monetary increase—
profit, pay, loan, usury, thrift, audit, treasure, legacy, bequest,
largess, bounty—are iterated throughout the series; and the
poet continues to warn against the self-retentive impulse that
will destroy the friend, presenting a single argument in a variety
of ingenious forms. To maintain such constant variation over a
hundred and fifty lines of verse without changing their basic
ideas proves an inventive wit not inferior to Donne's; but
although witty display is a strong stylistic element of the
Sonnets, there is a more important point to be taken here.
Shakespeare is clearly not concerned to tell a story; and whether
he is addressing an actual or an imaginary bachelor, he is using
the situation as the point of departure for a set of variations on a
theme. While this extended group of sonnets tells us almost
nothing about the young man, and contains no narrative
development at all, it reveals on a much larger scale the sort of
interest and intention that are implicit in Sonnets 153 and 154.

Shakespeare is taking a simple idea or situation, and writing about it from several slightly different points of view; varying either his attitude as commentator or the suggested circumstances of the young man's behaviour, and allowing his attention to move gradually towards adjacent ideas; but always developing the conceptual as distinct from the narrative potentialities of his theme.

By developing the situations of the Sonnets in this way, Shakespeare does not invite us to regard their story as fictional. But we may reasonably expect a true story, no less than an imaginary tale, to be consistent over points in detail and circumstance; and this the speaker of the sequence is not. In several cases a group of related poems is seen to contain a number of different, and perhaps alternative accounts of an event to which they are generally related; as though the poet's point of view were constantly shifting, and preventing him from fixing the terms of his subject. Examples of such inconsistency will be examined later in this chapter. It does not seem possible to reconcile such variation of circumstance with a narrative purpose, or with an actual experience. It might be argued that Shakespeare was deliberately obscuring the form of the event for diplomatic reasons, but such ambiguousness would puzzle the intended and the unauthorised reader alike. Moreover, such inconsistencies can be more simply explained. What is uncharacteristic of narrative is compatible with the writing of variant forms such as Sonnets 153 and 154 clearly represent. There is no definite idea of particular experience underlying the groups of related poems, for Shakespeare is evidently working out the form of an imaginative event by varying the circumstances which have prompted the poet to speak. The ideas of separation, neglect or weariness which act as linking themes within a group of sonnets might seem to have been suggested by the experiences which the poems describe; but it could be more exact to say that the story exists only by reason of Shakespeare's working-out of ideas which acquire form by being made to figure in a fictional relationship. Such development seems to be indicated where the later or final sonnets of a group offer a more completely realised expression of their common theme, and a more definite placing of the central event within a narrative context. The three sonnets 33–35 provide an example of such a gradual crystallising of initially vague concepts, where after some tentative movements towards alternative versions of a story, Shakespeare finds a more firmly shaped narrative episode to house the ideas imperfectly realised in the two previous poems.

The longest continuous run of sonnets is the series encouraging the young man to marry and reproduce his beauty. The poet's argument is maintained without interruption up to Sonnet 12, 'When I do count the clock', where the increase theme is almost crowded out of the poem by a new preoccupation. In the next sonnet increase is again the major subject; but although it recurs in Sonnet 16 and briefly in its successor, the theme has already ceased to be dominant. There are four other considerable groups of related sonnets. The first, on absence, begins with Sonnet 43 and continues with interruptions up to Sonnet 52. The second concerns a rival poet, who is first mentioned in Sonnet 79 and who drops out of the story after the superbly scornful Sonnet 86. The next poem introduces a prospect of separation which varies uncertainly between fact and likelihood until the massive statement of Sonnet 94 closes the issue. The fourth long group begins with the poet's self-rebuke of his silence in Sonnet 100, and continues through the apologies and explanations that follow, with some interruption, up to Sonnet 108. The other groups are generally much shorter than these, some consisting of only two sonnets. Of these, a few are linked head to tail, so that their argument runs on with no serious check over twenty-eight lines.

Of the individual sonnets in the sequence 1–126, many

contribute nothing to the story. Some, we have already seen, either speak impersonally or make no reference to the friend. We may suppose that Shakespeare occasionally wrote sonnets unconnected with his main theme of interest. Of the others, an appreciable number express reflections of a kind that might suggest themselves at any quiet moment, and without reference to a particular happening. Such a poem is Sonnet 59, 'If there be nothing new', or Sonnet 106, 'When in the chronicle of wasted time'. Both are addressed to the friend, but simply testify to the relationship and make no claim to be fitted into the sequence of events which other sonnets indicate. There remain what may for present purposes be called the load-bearing sonnets, which allude more or less specifically to the happenings which bring about changes and crises in the poet's relationship with his friend. The relationship seems to develop slowly at first. The opening sonnets are hortatory in tone and manner, and a hint of intimacy enters only at the end of Sonnet 10, in the poet's plea

> Make thee another self for love of me.

The hint is confirmed in Sonnet 13, where the poet addresses his friend as 'dear my love', and again two sonnets later in the poet's admission of being 'all in war with Time for love of you.' With Sonnet 18, 'Shall I compare thee', the poet's feelings reach the level of rapture, though nothing suggests that his affection is answered in the friend until the remark of Sonnet 22, that the friend's beauty

> Is but the seemly raiment of my heart,
> Which in thy breast doth live, as thine in me.

Even after this suggestion, which is supported by the plainer statement of Sonnet 25, 'I that love and am beloved', the sonnets continue to be preoccupied with the poet's devoted and some-times fearful love for the friend. If a relationship now exists, its current of feeling and attention seems to flow only in one direction; and the poet addresses a being so unresponsive and unmoving that he might be speaking to a beautiful effigy. However, the sequence 1–26 represents a heyday of kindly affection and assurance for the poet: the close friendship is unclouded by suspicion or foreboding, and the depression which will later attack him has still to show itself.

The opening phrase of Sonnet 27, 'Weary with toil', introduces a sombre mood and a new phase in the relationship. Together with the next poem, it also announces the first definite happening in the sketchy story. Whether the poet or the friend has gone away is not explained, but 'still farther off from thee' in Sonnet 28 shows that they are no longer together. This fragmentary piece of information is the first of fifteen references to events in the relationship which can be counted in the hundred poems that follow Sonnet 26. For present purposes it will be convenient to tabulate them, with a very general indication of their substance; remembering that this is not always clearly stated in the sonnets concerned. The order of events runs:

   (i) The poet is separated from his friend.   [27, 28]
  (ii) The friend disgraces himself and injures the poet, who forgives him and associates himself with his misdeed. [33–35]
 (iii) The friend betrays the poet by seducing his mistress: the poet again overlooks the injury.   [40–42]
 (iv) The poet makes a journey which separates him from the friend.   [50–52]
  (v) The friend neglects the poet, who watches the clock for him, knowing the friend to have found other company.   [57–58]
 (vi) Still neglected, the poet suffers from sleeplessness and is haunted by visions of the friend.   [61]
(vii) The friend is victimised by slanderous report, but reassured by the poet who sees envy as its cause. [70]

A different commentator might either add to this list or shorten
it, and might also disagree about the point at which any of
these topics dropped out of sight. Some latitude of interpretation is to be accepted where events are alluded to so indefinitely.
It is often uncertain at what point in the sequence a subject
which later emerges clearly has entered the field of discussion,
or where one topic shades off into another. To treat the sonnets
as though they contained well-defined clues to actual happenings, by bringing pressure to bear upon every hint of an event,
is to mistake the whole nature of their commentary. Their
matter is to a large extent in process of gestation, forming
itself as the poet works upon ideas that may be initially unresolved; and which in some groups of sonnets can be seen
taking shape, wavering and being replaced by an alternative
concept. If we suppose with Malone that Shakespeare had not
decided which of the two final sonnets to prefer, we should also

33

assume that some of the poems in the main sequence are alterna-
tives, offering versions of the same event which cannot stand
together in the same story. A reader who recognises how far the
Sonnets represent a working-out of ideas rather than a chron-
icling of fixed and actual events will not expect to be able to infer
anything about the circumstances of happenings that originate
in the process of the poet's intensive moulding and reshaping
of imaginative concepts.

So far as the story of the Sonnets can be analysed and dis-
cussed, it provides no very convincing account of the relationship that is its subject. The events, such as they are, have no
necessary or likely connection. The friend is absent on a journey;
he is the victim of slanderous report; the poet's talents are
temporarily eclipsed. Each event is separate from the other, and
the order in which they are presented is of no importance,
for they cannot be arranged to tell a continuous story. Where
there is reference to a common subject in a number of sonnets,
the inconsistency of report is sometimes great enough to suggest that the poet is not addressing the same friend throughout
the sequence. Thus, although Sonnet 41 reveals that the friend
has betrayed the poet, in Sonnet 92 the poet ruminates over the
friend's nature–'Thou mayst be false, and yet I know it not'–
as though there had been no earlier proof of inconstancy. But
in Sonnet 101 the friend is again an exemplar of virtue and
dependability, 'truth in beauty dyed'; and four sonnets later
the poet confesses that 'fair, kind and true' sums up all that
can be said of the young man. Such a change is not easily accountable if we hold that the Sonnets are concerned with
actual happenings. A poet perceptive enough to recognise
that the friend was relying on his beauty and charm to mask
viciousness of character would not be anxious to renew the
association which the friend callously breaks off; but in
Sonnet 97 he celebrates the young man's return, 'the pleasure
of the fleeting year', with uncritical enthusiasm for his

34

personal graces. Shakespeare had decided to put an unpleasant episode behind him, it might be suggested: but not to the extent of destroying the poems which comment upon it.

What emerges fairly clearly from the story is the general course of the relationship, which falls into three distinct phases. The first is the period of happy assurance which the poet might be recalling in Sonnet 102:

> Our love was new, and then but in the spring,
> When I was wont to greet it with my lays.

With Sonnet 27 the poet comes under strain from several different quarters, and his hold upon the friend's affections becomes progressively less secure. Two periods of absence help to indicate the growing rift between them; and after the poet has suffered neglect and deliberate unkindness he recognises in Sonnet 87 that he must reconcile himself to a final parting. Throughout this phase of their association the poet remains patient and endlessly forbearing; accepting without protest a series of affronts that vary between inconsiderateness and cruelty, and identifying himself with the friend to the extent of taking sides with him against himself. To some commentators the poet's behaviour has seemed spineless and contemptible: others have seen it as the noblest expression of selfless love. But the significance which should most concern us is imaginative, not moral; and perhaps this comes within reach when we recognise that in the third phase of the relationship, which begins with Sonnet 97, the previous positions of friend and poet are reversed. It is now the poet who apologises for misconduct and unkindness, and the friend whose 'most, most loving breast' must find excuses for the older man who has wilfully repudiated the ties of love and obligation by transferring his interests to other friends. The poet's admissions of shame and guilt, which are made intermittently between Sonnets 109 and

35

120, have a prelude in the four apologies for poetic silence in Sonnets 100–103; so that this third phase of the relationship is strongly coloured by the poet's efforts to make amends for unkind or neglectful behaviour very much like the friend's had been previously. The parallel is noted in Sonnet 120, 'That you were once unkind', where the poet acknowledges how their former positions are reversed:

> For if you were by my unkindness shaken
> As I by yours, y'have passed a hell of time;
> And I, a tyrant, have no leisure taken
> To weigh how once I suffered in your crime.

One might comment that for the unshakeably constant poet of the earlier sonnets to behave as he now describes must require a complete metamorphosis of character; but the story is not to be taken so seriously. The reversal of positions which makes the patient sufferer of the second phase of relationship the abject and inexcusable wrongdoer of the third is a form of rhetorical device, which Shakespeare applies to narrative as to figures of speech. The recurrent commonplace of the poet's argument that he is his friend, to a degree which makes self-interest the implementing of the friend's wishes, is finally embodied in the variations which put the poet almost literally in the friend's place. At several points of the sequence the poet is made to duplicate the friend's behaviour or experience in this way. The friend goes on a journey in Sonnets 27–28, the poet in Sonnets 50–52. The friend is the victim of slanderous report in Sonnet 70, and the poet is similarly stigmatised in Sonnet 121. Where the friend renders the poet incapable of writing by transferring his patronage to a rival, the poet subsequently silences his own habitual praise of the friend by transferring his attention to a similarly unworthy figure. Such correspondences are directed by the same purpose as we see working within groups of related sonnets, exploiting an element of story which

serves primarily as a basis for Shakespeare's imaginative interrogation of identity.

It is the separateness of these two linked figures which the
story of the Sonnets urges upon us repeatedly; or rather, the
poet's unrelaxing anxiety not to become detached from the
friend with whom he identifies himself. After the short happy
period of assurance at the beginning of the story, there are few
moments when the prospect of separation or alienation does
not hang over the poet. During the absence of either, the poet
feels a distress that is not much relieved when he or the friend
returns. There are obstacles to the friendship; the 'separable
spite' of Sonnet 36, a characteristically indefinite allusion to a
force which prevents their meeting as often as the poet would
like; and premonitory fears of losing the friend to a less
devoted admirer. With these are the growing signs of indifference deepening to undisguised contempt as the friend
recognises the modesty of the poet's gifts and social rank, and
turns to more exciting company. Acknowledging his limitations, the poet does not resist the friend's withdrawal of favour
but offers to help in repudiating himself; even here trying to
insist upon their kinship by associating himself unreservedly
with the friend's heartless purpose. His frequent confession of
being tongue-tied and unable to address the friend reveals in a
homely way how the poet is frustrated in his wish to establish
a close and permanent relationship with him. The poet's Muse
fails him, and the friend yields to the attraction of more voluble
writers whose flamboyance strikes the poet dumb. Later, when
the poet himself is guilty of inconstancy and neglect, the same
problem of maintaining contact with the friend recurs in
another form: he has wasted his affection, or his literary talent,
upon some rival interest, and must now convince the injured
friend that his remorse and shame are heartfelt. There are from
time to time moments of assurance and inward calm, when the
poet speaks of his love with a pride that is reflected in the

measured dignity of the verse-movement; but the predominant emotion of the Sonnets varies between anxiety and depression, as the poet reaches for a contentment that repeatedly eludes him.

Critics who see in the Sonnets a direct account of Shakespeare's personal experiences are not usually nonplussed by the vagueness of the poet's allusions to happenings in the story, and seem to find no difficulty in determining the year and the particular circumstances in which the events occurred. Thus if the poet writes of being away from the friend, we may recognise an allusion to a provincial tour forced upon Shakespeare's company by an outbreak of plague in London; and as the number of sonnets indicates an absence of some weeks, they were written during a prolonged closure of the playhouses in 1597. Such an assumption might have a limited validity if it could also be shown that the poet of the Sonnets is Shakespeare himself. The only factual information which the sonnets in question provide is that the poet is riding away from his friend. It is obviously important to restrain fanciful hypothesis, and to pay strictly respectful attention to what the Sonnets do, and do not, tell us. Their meaning is imaginatively implicit; and the terms which must concern the critic are those which Shakespeare has used to denote his imaginative purposes, not the biographical glosses which a commentator substitutes for them.

Such attempts to read episodes of Shakespeare's personal life into the Sonnets help to obscure the indefiniteness that is part of their poetic character, and to ignore the points of narrative inconsistency which provide a truer indication of what the poems represent. Dowden's comment on the group of four poems beginning with Sonnet 100 reveal how completely this readiness to see Shakespeare in every line can blind the critic to what is actually said. These four poems were composed, he suggests, after a cessation from sonnet-writing, during which Shakespeare had been engaged in authorship—writing plays for the public, as I suppose, instead of poems for his friend.

The sonnets concerned, Dowden also supposes, constitute Shakespeare's personal utterance; and since Shakespeare was a dramatist as well as a sonneteer, the stage must have been responsible for his neglect of the young man. Dowden should have noticed that the poet of the Sonnets nowhere refers to himself as a dramatist, and that only one of his images suggests a familiarity with the playhouse. He should also have recognised that although they all admit that the friend has been neglected, the four sonnets do not agree that the poet has stopped writing altogether. When the poet first alludes to the topic he implies that he has been wasting his energy on a trivial subject:

> Spend'st thou thy fury on some worthless song,
> Dark'ning thy power to lend base subjects light?
> [100

This is an unlikely reference to dramatic writing; for even if the phrase 'base subjects' were taken as a hit at the groundlings, the plays are not to be seen as 'song'; a term used in several sonnets in the conventional literary sense. Sonnet 101 confirms that the friend has been forgotten when it speaks of the poet's 'neglect of beauty dyed'; but it does not renew the suggestion that the poet has been distracted by some unworthy interest. It now seems that the poet has written nothing at all. By challenging his inactive Muse,

> Because he needs no praise, wilt thou be dumb?
> Excuse not silence so;

the poet protects himself against a possible rebuke from the friend, not of disloyalty but of unproductiveness. Of the two other poems in this group, Sonnet 102 leaves it uncertain whether the poet has stopped writing altogether, or has severely reduced his output. 'I love not less, though less the show appear,' suggests that his poetic compliments have become fewer and less effusive; but the comparison with the nightingale who 'stops her pipe' implies more than this. A remark in the couplet, 'I sometimes hold my tongue', leaves the question open: does the poet fall silent for a day or two, or for a whole season? The next variation on the theme takes up a more definite position. The poet complains that he has been deserted by his Muse, and appeals to the friend for tolerance:

O blame me not if I no more can write!
[103

The friend's beauty is responsible for his silence, the poet explains; for he is put to shame by the wretched efforts of his 'blunt invention' to do justice to such a theme, and prefers to suppress either the attempt or its lifeless product.

Dowden's reading of these four sonnets involves two errors. His assumption that the poet–whether Shakespeare or not–had ceased from sonnet-writing is open to argument. Two sonnets speak explicitly of the poet's silence; another is ambiguous, and the fourth suggests that he has been writing 'some worthless song': worthless evidently because its praises were directed upon an undeserving object, and not–as Dowden seems to think–because it was a play. There would be better justification, in a literal interpretation of the Sonnets, for supposing that the poet had been addressing sonnets elsewhere. Where the story is in fact confused, Dowden writes as though all four sonnets told the same tale. His second error lies in supposing that the poet's tributes have dried up because he had, reluctantly, to supply his company with a play. It is wrong to assume that Shakespeare is here speaking of himself, wrong to twist the phrase 'worthless song' into meaning a trivial play, and wrong to suggest that the poet's explanations stop there.

40

Each of the sonnets of the group offers its own account of what has happened:

(i) The poet's Muse has been playing truant and wasting inspiration on a trivial theme: it must now return and redeem time 'so idly spent.'

(ii) The Muse has recognised that such beauty stands in no need of praise, and has not sought to address the friend.

(iii) The poet's love is unchanged, despite appearances: if he writes less, or not at all, it is to prevent his poetry becoming wearisome to the friend.

(iv) The poet has realised that his attempts to describe the friend are futile: his beauty surpasses all that poetry could say, and makes the attempt itself seem perverse.

The first of these explanations supports Dowden's assumption, but the others clearly do not; for the good reason that they are not discussing the same circumstance. The only common ground which the four poems share is their attempt to explain or excuse the poet's neglect of a patron. Their individual treatment of this theme involves disparity and inconsistency great enough to make it doubtful not merely whether any such situation ever arose, but whether Shakespeare had proposed it to himself in definite terms. The differences between these four accounts of what purports to be a single situation suggests that he did not; and that he took the theme of silence as motif about which to shape the variations which Dowden has read as a single report.

The third variation, Sonnet 102, deserves attention for its unusual deftness and emotional restraint as well as for its explanation, which is quite unlike the other three. The poem carries a guarded yet palpable hint that the poet is rebuking the friend's incomplete appreciation of the tributes paid to him;

although earlier he has been credited with an ear 'that doth thy lays esteem.' The general dignity of the poem helps to give the remark, 'I would not dull you with my song', the sense of a courteous but firm announcement that the poet does not intend to waste endeavour upon an unappreciative audience. The creative spirit which was described as either 'resty,' 'forgetful' or 'truant' in the two preceding sonnets now appears to have none of these qualities: the poet is deliberately withholding the utterance he might otherwise make, knowing that he cannot expect a proper hearing. If it were necessary to pick out one of these four poems as the 'true' explanation of the poet's silence, Sonnet 102 would be the obvious choice; for unlike the others it avoids rhetorical flourish and offers a simple argument based on feeling, not wit. No such choice is required of us; for inconsistencies between sonnet and sonnet do not mean that some are true and some false, but that all are variants based on a common theme. There is no conflict of fact over the cause and degree of the poet's silence, but four versions of an explanation to the friend. The poet has in turn been entirely unproductive, has written little, or has transferred his interests to another literary subject; he has wilfully neglected the friend, he is incapable of praising him, he has deliberately reduced the number of poems addressed to him. He admonishes his Muse for glorifying an unworthy object, he apologises for its speechlessness, and he refers to his writing as an activity which he controls at will. Each sonnet modifies a common theme as the poet takes a new standpoint and varies his persona; neither giving a fuller account of a single situation nor developing a story, but working out intensively a fresh aspect of the relationship between poet and friend.

These four sonnets have a fixed central idea in the notion of the poet's silence. Other groups of related sonnets look towards a shifting centre. As a group they treat a more or less common subject; but their variations on this shared theme involve changes of circumstance in the narrative background to which they refer, so that as Shakespeare steadily works over his main concept, the outline of his story alters its shape, and it becomes impossible to determine exactly why the relationship of poet and friend has changed. The run of sonnets beginning with Sonnet 87 provides an example. Dover Wilson's proposal to call them 'the Farewell Sonnets' is justified by the allusions to parting which figure in six consecutive poems, though with varying emphasis. The argument for including Sonnets 93 and 94 with this group is not convincing. In Sonnet 93 the poet's interests seem to be shading off towards a new topic, and Sonnet 94 constitutes a magisterial *pronunciamento* separated from its neighbours by its impersonality as well as by its tone of massive authority. Setting these two aside, the unifying theme of the group is explicitly stated in the first line of Sonnet 87,

> Farewell: thou art too dear for my possessing.

The friend, it appears from what follows, has had second thoughts about the fitness of his association with the poet; and 'on better judgement making' he has decided to withdraw his familiar patronage. The poet recognises that he has no proper grounds of complaint over this loss: nothing entitles him to so rich a possession as the friend, and he cannot pretend to deserve such favour as the young man has hitherto granted him. It follows that the friend must discover his mistake and revoke his kindness:

> The cause of this fair gift in me is wanting,
> And so my patent back again is swerving.

By insisting upon his own worthlessness and the friend's great importance, the poet makes it appear inevitable that they should separate, without any blame falling upon the young man in ending their association. The next sonnet presents a quite different state of affairs. It begins by envisaging a future time

> When thou shalt be disposed to set me light,
>   [88

and continues to speak as though the friendship were in no
immediate danger of being dissolved. The poem may hint at
the speaker's suspicion that his relationship with the young man
is deteriorating, and that he must prepare some defence
against unkindness to come; but the break which seems
to be the accompanying event of Sonnet 87 is here merely
in prospect. The poet's mood has also changed. The directness of 'set me light', whose suggestion of injustice contrasts
with the poet's unprotesting modesty in the previous sonnet,
and an explicit reference to his deserts in the second line of
Sonnet 88,

> And place my merit in the eye of scorn,

show a readiness to challenge his undervaluation by the friend.
If there is a sense of indignation here, it probably persists in the
poet's equivocal promise to 'prove thee virtuous, though thou
art forsworn'; but unless the poet is assuming that this pros-
pective event can be regarded as inevitable, he must mean not
'Although in fact you have betrayed me', but 'Even if you
should have broken your word.' The argument of the sonnet—
a promise to justify the friend's ill-treatment by taking his part—
is an encouragement to adopt the second reading. There has
been no desertion and no betrayal; but if the poet were ever
to be rejected, he would publicly approve the friend's faith-
lessness, deliberately bringing dishonour upon himself by
disclosing hidden faults, and so doing credit to the young man's
good judgement in casting him off:

> That thou in losing me shalt win much glory.

The poet will also gain by this action; for if these self-inflicted injuries are to the friend's advantage they must benefit the poet, who loves him more than himself.

This second variation on the theme of farewell outlines a different situation. In Sonnet 87 the poet speaks after the friendship has collapsed, and he has newly learned that he has possessed the friend only 'as a dream doth flatter.' The legal terminology of his argument suggests that he now appreciates how flimsy his right to this possession had been. Sonnet 88 presents the situation in quite different terms. There is no crisis in the relationship, which remains firm and not obviously in hazard; and the poet is merely contemplating the possibility of losing the friend's regard. If he should ever be repudiated, the poet will not only accept his separation from the friend as inevitable, but will actively help him to justify his betrayal of the poet's trust. The speaker's promise, 'Against myself I'll fight', is one of several comments which show him to be discussing a hypothetical situation, and not dealing with an actual rupture. In Sonnet 89, where the poet has been rejected, Shakespeare returns to the original state of affairs; but instead of developing the argument previously advanced in Sonnet 87, he makes the poet vary his promise to lend support to the friend's unkindness. He will now corroborate whatever slanderous accusation the friend chooses to make:

> Say that thou didst forsake me for some fault
> And I will comment upon that offence;
> Speak of my lameness, and I straight will halt,
> Against thy reasons making no defence.

Knowing that the friend wishes to be dissociated from him will be enough to impel the poet to act against his personal interests. He will take more pleasure in gratifying the friend's wish not to see him than in satisfying his own yearning for the friend's company:

I will acquaintance strangle and look strange,
Be absent from thy walks, and in my tongue
Thy sweet beloved name no more shall dwell,
Lest I—too much profane—should do it wrong.

Sonnet 90 presents yet another variation on the theme. The poet
has not been discarded; but, as in Sonnet 88, he seems to have
some premonition that the friend is about to break off their
association. Already distressed by misfortune, he appeals to the
friend not to withhold the culminating blow which he seems to
have planned:

If thou wilt leave me, do not leave me last,
When other petty griefs have done their spite,
But in the onset come; so shall I taste
At first the very worst of fortune's might.

The poem does not reveal clearly whether the poet knows that
the friendship is about to be dissolved, and is asking for a rapid
coup de grâce, or whether he is telling the friend, 'If you should
ever wish to inflict a crowning misfortune on me, now would
be the most fitting moment.' What is not in doubt, in this
poem as in Sonnet 88, is the fact that the event is in prospect
only; for throughout the poet uses the future tense to discuss
the happening which may come about. As Sonnets 87 and 89
tell a different story, the reader faces a conflict of circumstance
over a point important enough to Shakespeare—were he relating
an actual experience—to have reported without contradicting
himself. Those who prefer to regard the Sonnets as private
autobiography can resolve the anomaly by arranging the four
poems in a different sequence, and by assuming that the two
apprehensive sonnets were written before the break alluded to
in Sonnets 87 and 89 had occurred. Dover Wilson adopts
this solution, and identifies Sonnet 91 as the initial poem of a
group written 'after Shakespeare's admission of defeat by the
learned Chapman ... and in anticipation of the inevitable

breach recorded in 87.' But the group of sonnets written around this 'inevitable breach' contains other inconsistencies which are not accounted for by rearranging their order. The obviously central issue of whether the poet felt himself betrayed by a trusted friend, or saw the friendship dissolve as both he and the young man realised their incompatibility of status, remains in doubt whatever the order of the sonnets in this group. In this respect they tell as contradictory a story as the previous group of poems, which turns about the theme of the poet's silence without reaching any definite conclusion about the extent of his inactivity or its cause. Such disagreement over circumstances is a characteristic feature of the groups of sonnets which, for some critics, constitute fixed points of Shakespeare's narrative. The variations of detail which such groups contain challenge this view. A writer describing the course of his deeply-felt attachment to a friend would be unlikely to contradict himself so habitually over matters of vital fact.

There may be some encouragement to regard Sonnet 91 as initiating the 'farewell' group in its quieter treatment of the theme, as though the poet had not yet warmed to his subject. Alternatively, after being vigorously explored in the four preceding sonnets, its interest has waned; and Shakespeare's attention is moving to an adjoining topic. The idea of separation does not appear until the closing lines of Sonnet 91, after the poet has admitted that he values the friend's affection more than any other possession. He then remarks,

> thou mayst take
> All this away, and me most wretched make.

After this short reference to the possibility of losing the friend, the next sonnet picks up the argument immediately by beginning,

> But do thy worst to steal thyself away;
> For term of life thou art assured mine.

This introduces a new variation of idea. Previously the poet has responded to the fact or the prospect of being discarded (i) without surprise, acknowledging that he could expect nothing else, (ii) by offering to help the friend repudiate and discredit him, (iii) by promising to meet the friend's wishes by avoiding even the mention of his name, and (iv) by encouraging the friend to deliver his blow at once. The fifth sonnet of this sequence reaches the idea of desertion too late to develop any new proposal; but its sequel in Sonnet 92 presents an argument parallel to the others. The poet now comments that (v) since his life depends upon the friend's love, the prospect of being rejected–'the worst of wrongs'–need not disturb him, for a much smaller injury would prove fatal. But this sonnet is not altogether of a piece with the others. Although the poet continues to declare his love, and to assert that he cannot survive without the friend's answering affection, he no longer promises to disregard his private interests by concealing the friend's disloyalty. Instead, he revives the hint of indignation given in Sonnet 88, and modifies his usually respectful tone of address to show something like scorn for the friend's capricious feelings:

> I see a better state to me belongs
> Than that which on thy humour doth depend:
> Thou canst not vex me with inconstant mind

–because, the poet explains, such treatment would kill him. Emotionally, he is at the mercy of the friend's whims, and glad to remind himself that he cannot outlive the pain of being discarded; but this extravagant admission of dependence upon the friend's kindness is acidly qualified by the critical evaluation of his shallow purposes: 'thy humour . . . inconstant mind.' Taken at its face value, the sonnet seems to profess the same complete dependence upon the young man as many earlier poems; but these loaded phrases call attention to the equivocal attitude which the poet is now taking up. The friend–and perhaps the reader–can be expected to read this elaborate tribute with no suspicion of its sincerity; but beneath a show of unchanged adoration which accepts the young man's vicious and unworthy traits without protest, the poet is beginning to show his teeth. If the friendship is to dissolve, the breach could be caused not by the young man's disloyalty but by the poet's growing contempt for his waywardness.

If we adopt the suggestion that this poem was written before Sonnet 87, we shall have to account for a radical change of attitude in the poet after this scornful allusion to the friend's inconstancy, and his ambiguously worded resolution not to be disturbed by the friend's whims. But it is hard to reconcile his appreciation in Sonnet 87,

> thou art too dear for my possessing,

with the more realistic recognition of Sonnet 92 that the friend's affection is shallow and capricious, and that the poet is not obliged to wait upon his uncertain favour. It might seem reasonable to reverse the order of these two poems on the ground that the separation which is apparently just happening in the first is being contemplated in the second as a future possibility; but as Sonnet 92 shows a discerning judgement lacking in Sonnet 87, there are equally good grounds for leaving their order unchanged. The later poem brings this group of sonnets to an end by allowing the poet to realise that he may be more seriously deceived in the young man than he has supposed:

> Thou mayst be false, and yet I know it not.

His thought is immediately taken up in Sonnet 93, which turns its attention upon the enigma of a face too beautiful to betray evil impulse, and says nothing about separation. From an allusion to the friend's duplicity, 'Thy looks with me, thy heart in other place', it seems that the poet is still admitted as a close acquaintance; but the point has no significance. Shakespeare's interest has moved to a new centre of ideas, and is now occupied with a theme whose power over his imaginative outlook is more strongly marked: the disquieting possibility that virtuous appearance may prove mere show without substance. The late sonnets of the 'farewell' group do not lead backwards to a narrative sequel in Sonnet 87, but merge gradually with the interests of a group which follow theirs, whose key-word might be 'show.'

A further group of associated sonnets is made up by the four poems which begin with Sonnet 33. Some hesitation might be felt over taking them as a group; for their common theme is not announced in the first of the four sonnets, and must be inferred from more explicit parallel statements in the second and third poems of the group. Sonnet 35, which begins

No more be grieved at that which thou hast done;

makes it clear that the friend has dishonoured himself by a slip whose nature is suggested in a reference to his 'sensual fault.' Reading backwards from this disclosure we may recognise more guarded allusions to the subject in Sonnet 34, where the poet speaks of 'thy shame' and describes himself bearing 'the strong offence's cross.' In Sonnet 35 his treatment of the subject is almost wholly figurative, and his allusions to the friend's misdeed and his own injury are so cryptic that, without the help of the two following sonnets, they might remain doubtful. Taken together, these three sonnets produce an impression of gradually clearing obscurity, where after cautiously figurative references to sunshine and storm the poet sets diplomatic reserve aside and speaks more plainly of what has happened. From this impression it might be inferred that in the immediate shock of disillusion the writer cannot bring himself to comment directly upon the event; and that when he discusses the subject openly in Sonnet 35 he has both regained his balance and recaptured the generous love that can forgive his erring friend. This assumes that the situation described in Sonnet 35 exists, so to speak, behind the two preceding sonnets; and that in writing them Shakespeare, as a party concerned, knew what particular events they refer to so allusively.

The alternative assumption is that Shakespeare–now considered simply as poet, and not as an actor in the 'story' of the Sonnets–is feeling his way towards the situation outlined in Sonnet 35; and that this situation has no more implicit existence behind the two previous poems than Hamlet has when he is off-stage. In the third sonnet Shakespeare realises the conception vaguely indicated in the preceding pair, by fitting his two figures into a situation which represents his ideas in substantial form. It is this eventual realising of concepts less successfully presented in Sonnets 33 and 34 which seems to be reflected in the calmly controlled manner and directness of Sonnet 35. Before trying to follow the development of these ideas, it will be helpful to have a clear grasp of the situation which this third sonnet describes.

Its initial consolation, 'No more be grieved at that which thou hast done,' is supported by parallel examples of beauty blemished or corrupted which run to the end of line 4. The poet then continues:

> All men make faults, and even I in this,
> Authorising thy trespass with compare;
> Myself corrupting, salving thy amiss;
> Excusing thy sins more than thy sins are.

The poet too is at fault; in finding parallels which justify the friend's slip, and in trying to charm away his evidently well-deserved sense of guilt. His search for excuses is more reprehensible than the friend's misconduct, since it involves a wilful misuse of moral judgement. He goes on:

For to thy sensual fault I bring in sense:
Thy adverse party is thy advocate;
And 'gainst myself a lawful plea commence.

Interpretation of this passage turns upon the allusion to the friend's 'sensual fault.' The obvious way of glossing the phrase is to assume that the poet is speaking of the lasciviousness which he attributes to the friend in Sonnet 40, where the friend has stolen the poet's mistress; and to argue that Sonnet 35 should stand with the adjacent group of poems treating this subject. This proposal is attractive only if we accept that the Sonnets tell a more or less coherent story, that their matter relates to actual happenings, and that those poems which have a common or closely similar narrative element should be grouped together. If we see the Sonnets as variations on themes of relationship we shall not suppose that the two groups, 33–35 and 40–42, have the same subject; but that the second group represents a re-working of the ideas progressively educed in the first, where the figure of the mistress has still to appear. It may be wrong to assume that 'sensual' in Sonnet 35 implies promiscuity, which has this concealed meaning in Sonnet 141; though its appearance in the earlier poem may mark the point at which Shakespeare began to think forward into the situation developed by Sonnets 40–42. Whatever conclusion we reach about the intentions of 'sensual' in Sonnet 35 must risk being invalidated by the play on words to which it contributes. If it was chosen partly for this punning effect, Shakespeare is unlikely to have intended 'sensual' to bear the significance sometimes drawn from it. Something much simpler could be meant. 'As defence counsel I engage sense [= my intellect] to plead on behalf of your sensual fault [= misdeed caused by thoughtless impulse]'; it being further proof of the poet's corruptness that he perverts reason in this fashion. The friend's 'adverse party', the poet whom he has injured, confounds common sense by acting as the young man's advocate; which puts him in the absurd position of conducting a case against his own interests. The sonnet concludes:

> Such civil war is in my love and hate
> That I an accessary needs must be
> To that sweet thief which sourly robs from me.

Perhaps this allusion to robbery should be understood as an early and indirect reference to the theft reported in Sonnet 40, where the same gentle thief appears to have stolen the poet's mistress. But in the three sonnets concerned with this incident, the poet does not speak plainly of the liaison between his friend and the mistress until the closing lines of the second poem, Sonnet 41; so that if Sonnets 33–35 allude to the same theft, Shakespeare takes up four and almost five of these six related poems in making a devious approach to the disclosure of Sonnet 42, 'That thou hast her'; where at last he reveals unambiguously what has happened. What purpose could this obliqueness be intended to serve? If the Sonnets are addressed to an actual friend, he would be no less aware of his theft than the wronged poet. Are we to suppose that Shakespeare broke the news gently to his friend that he knew of the liaison, by sending him each of the six poems separately, each hinting more broadly at the truth? The sonnets themselves create an altogether different impression. They suggest that the poet begins with only a vague awareness of the incident which comes into focus with Sonnet 42. The imprecise suggestions of Sonnets 33–35 become less tentative not because the poet speaks out more plainly, but because Shakespeare is working them out. Inconsistencies in the narrative arise where the poet makes an approach to his theme which subsequently he varies or discards.

The successive stages of such an imaginative development are simply laid out in Sonnets 33–35. The exact nature of the friend's 'trespass' is not explained in any of the three poems; but from Sonnet 35, the most informative of them, we gather that he has dishonoured himself and injured the poet by a 'sensual fault' which, however obscure, must involve a surrender to impulse; and that the poet forgives him so completely that he is ready to defend the young man's misconduct. Very little of this could be gathered from Sonnet 33. From the analogy which occupies the octet it appears that the friend's earlier splendour has been darkened by a disgrace wilfully brought upon himself:

> Anon permit the basest clouds to ride
> With ugly rack on his celestial face.

Nothing suggests that the poet has suffered any personal loss other than by parting company with an idealised conception of his friend:

> But out, alack, he was but one hour mine;
> The region cloud hath masked him from me now.

However the friend has disgraced himself, he has not injured the poet directly by theft or betrayal. The poet is disillusioned, but able to re-establish his love by arguing that the noblest virtue may suffer eclipse no less than the beauty of the sun:

> Suns of the world may stain, when heaven's sun staineth.

In short, then, Sonnet 33 implies a very simple situation. The friend has committed some dishonourable act, and the poet's belief in his untarnished nobility has been shattered. He reconciles himself to the facts, and reaffirms his love for the young man. The next sonnet retains the main elements of this situation. The poet speaks again of suffering a painful disappointment in the friend, and of coming to terms with a transformed state of affairs; but from this common basis Shakespeare develops a quite different line of feeling. The speaker's opening question shows him puzzled and resentful at the friend's inconsiderate treatment, which has dashed his happy expectation of enjoying a secure relationship:

Why didst thou promise such a beauteous day,
And let me travel forth without my cloak;
To let base clouds o'ertake me in my way,
Hiding thy bravery in their rotten smoke?

[34

The poet is no longer a bystander involved in the young man's disgrace through ties of affection, but the victim of the young man's callousness. His commentary is no more explicit about the nature of this 'ill deed' than about the disgrace of Sonnet 33; but since the onlooker has now become the victim, the two misdeeds cannot be the same. This suggests that the 'trespass' referred to in Sonnet 35, which follows, is another variant of an idea common to all three poems. More new circumstances follow the opening complaint of Sonnet 34. The friend has apologised and tried to make amends for his unkindness to the poet; unsuccessfully, for the poet is not yet disposed to forget his hurt. ' 'Tis not enough,' he tells the friend,

that through the cloud thou break
To dry the rain on my storm-beaten face;
For no man well of such a salve can speak
That heals the wound and cures not the disgrace.

It is not now the young man but the friend who bears the stigma of dishonour, as though the guilt of one were transferable to the other. The issue of the poet's disgrace is extended into the next four lines, but with no indication of its cause:

Nor can thy shame give physic to my grief;
Though thou repent, yet I have still the loss:
The offender's sorrow lends but weak relief
To him that bears the strong offence's cross.

The poet's 'cross' could be identical with the 'disgrace' of l. 8; but unless 'the loss' means loss of good name or public respect,

55

the poet must be referring to a form of injury not previously mentioned. The sense of his initial complaint is that the friend has encouraged the poet to expect favour and patronage, but has in fact humiliated him. By apologising he has taken away the sting of the poet's disappointment, but he has not been able to restore the public standing lost by the poet in being made to look ridiculous. On this reading, the poet's allusions to his injury have a single intention; and the 'loss' admitted in this sonnet is not to be associated with the theft which he encourages 'that sweet thief' to commit in the next poem.

Sonnet 34 ends with an emotional volte-face as the friend breaks into tears and the poet, unable to sustain his resentment, reverts to the attitude of uncritical love typical of him. Developing this situation, Sonnet 35 opens naturally by offering the friend comfort in the distress which he now feels:

> No more be grieved at that which thou hast done.

His well-intentioned reminder that 'all men make faults' leads to the reference to the friend's 'sensual fault' which, like all the allusions to misdeeds in this group of sonnets, seems inexplicit by design. The only clear inference that can be drawn from the phrase is that it does not refer to the inconsiderate behaviour ascribed to the friend in Sonnet 34, but to a more serious moral lapse. Evidently Shakespeare has returned to the situation described in the first sonnet of the group, where the young man has brought disgrace upon himself and disillusion to the poet. There are obvious differences: the poet has absorbed the painful realisation that 'loathsome canker lives in sweetest bud', and can argue against moral integrity in the interests of his friend's peace of mind; and he is no longer an onlooker as in Sonnet 33, but a party damaged by his friend's actions. He is not, however, a plaintiff, as in the previous poem, but in his own words an accessory to the young man's crime; seeking to palliate its

gravity although himself injured by it. The development of
this theme from Sonnet 33 takes the following course:

(i) The friend dishonours himself by misconduct. The poet
is not directly involved, but is temporarily disillusioned
in the friend.

(ii) The friend treats the poet shabbily, making him publicly
ridiculous after promising him favour or patronage. He
apologies, but cannot remove the disgrace; and the poet
remains resentful until softened by the friend's tears.

(iii) The friend disgraces himself by misconduct which also
injures the poet, who encourages him to forget this
lapse but admits that his argument is as reprehensible
as the friend's misdeed.

A summary helps to show that the two situations either described or implicit in Sonnets 34 and 35 are incompatible with
that of Sonnet 33; and that although some likeness exists between
(ii) and (iii), there are inconsistencies in the suggested nature of
the friend's misdeed and in the poet's attitude towards his
lapse, which in (ii) involves only the poet in disgrace. It is clear
that the incidents represented by (i) and (ii) cannot form parts of
the same story. Their common use of sunshine-and-storm
imagery links them imaginatively, but from this shared ground
they diverge to give accounts of two different though similar
events, of which the second is the more definite. Those who
read the Sonnets as autobiography assume that the argument
of Sonnet 35, in which the poet associates himself with the
friend's misdeed by condoning his moral fault, is the narrative
sequel to the reconciliation described in the previous poem.
The general tendency of ideas in the two poems encourages
this view, and their association through related concepts is not
in dispute. Hostility between the poet and his friend gives way
to a renewal of affection, and the poet springs to the defence of

a crime which he knows to be culpable, as love for the friend proves stronger than self-interest. But in their details the two sonnets do not tally. Instead of the consistent development that a single story would display, the three poems of this group have the diversity typical of poems written on an imaginative theme, where the poet is free to exploit the potentialities of his motif in a variety of forms, without binding himself to the fixed conditions of an actual situation or event.

Such inconsistencies occurring within so many groups of related sonnets should make it impossible to believe that Shakespeare is describing his own experiences, or even telling a connected or purposeful story. Some occasional self-contradiction or vagueness over matters of detail might be expected of an extended narrative, especially when it is related in a medium ill-adapted to story-telling. But the anomalies in the poet's story—if we can accept this term—go well beyond this kind of irregularity. Major and minor divergences over circumstances and happenings occur in every considerable group of sonnets; each poem sometimes giving its own version of an event whose form is nowhere precisely defined, and whose actors may exchange roles in different accounts of the occurrence. Instead of building upon the story indicated by one sonnet and supplying more details, its sequel outlines a rather different state of affairs and sets its characters in a new relationship. A third sonnet of the group may agree with neither, or confirm parts of both previous versions of the event. Jointly, such linked sonnets may leave an impression of a situation whose exact terms have still to be worked out, and which are currently in a fluid state. The poet seems to have a general sense of the conditions which he intends to explore, but not to have committed himself by fixing its circumstances in advance. The elements of the narrative situation are treated as movable, adaptable counters, to be shifted into fresh positions or exchanged for similar figures as the poet tries to give stabilised form to concepts which are

the basic material of the Sonnets. He never reaches this point of
fully resolved expression; for the stuff which Shakespeare
manipulates is not inert, but the product of an imaginative
activity which, as he works upon it, continues to develop
beyond his reach.

CHAPTER THREE

The Poet

To those who read the Sonnets as a story involving actual people, the identity of the poet presents no problems. The friend, the rival poet, and the 'woman coloured ill' are all cryptic figures who have aroused curiosity and prompted speculation since the Sonnets were first held to be a work of autobiography. Attempts to identify them still continue. The figure of the poet has excited no such inquiry. To the literalists it has always been self-evident that the poet who narrates the story of his two loves is the same poet who wrote the Sonnets, and that when he speaks of himself he is speaking about Shakespeare. There is in fact no *prima facie* reason for making this assumption; and it is not easy to understand how such a belief has been able to establish itself. That the story is told in the first person proves nothing; but commentators continue to write as though this narrative mode were exclusive to autobiography, and forbidden to fiction. To argue that the self-portrait is unmistakable in 'the generous instincts, the susceptibility to beauty, the moral discrimination, the enthusiasm' which the Sonnets display, amounts only to supposing that Shakespeare possessed the attractive human qualities which seem appropriate to a great poet. His admirers would find the same qualities in the plays; but criticism has developed beyond the level of reading Shakespeare into his dramatic characters, or of attributing to Shakespeare personally the human attributes of his more appealing figures. If he is Hamlet, he is also Pompey and Caliban. However much we know about the character of Shakespeare's work, the personal identity of its author remains in the dark to us; and it is impossible to demonstrate a link between that unknown being and the poet whose enigmatic experiences are described in the Sonnets. Without some independent knowledge of Shakespeare's personal qualities, we have no means of showing that the Sonnets reflect his temperament and outlook; and no grounds for supposing that Shakespeare is speaking of himself in their narrator.

However, we possess some factual information about the general course of Shakespeare's life and career; and if the Sonnets were indeed autobiographical we might expect them to refer to events and circumstances in the poet's life known to us from other sources. There would then be some reason to regard the speaker of the Sonnets as Shakespeare, and to find a reflection of his personal character in their commentary. In this respect the Sonnets are unhelpful. The speaker nowhere refers unambiguously to an event or experience which we know Shakespeare to have undergone. Few happenings of any kind are mentioned, and those in such vague terms that their meaning is in dispute. There are no unmistakable references to Shakespeare's work as a dramatist; and although the speaker repeatedly alludes to his writing of poetry, it does not appear that he has published two narrative poems with considerable success. To the contrary, he describes himself as an ungifted and outdated poet whose work is largely disregarded, and which could appeal to his patron only through its simple sincerity. He complains of suffering misfortune and public disgrace, and while Shakespeare's life is too poorly chronicled for its exigencies to be known, no contemporary allusion suggests that he encountered difficulties of this kind; and likelihoods seem against it. Not only do the Sonnets disclose a chapter of the poet's life whose events are unrelated to anything we know of Shakespeare: they depict a writer whose comments about himself, and whose seeming exclusion from the world of affairs in which Shakespeare actually moved, must suggest that some other person is their narrator.

The belief that Shakespeare himself is the speaker throughout
the sequence has been encouraged by some of the narrator's
references to his art as a poet; in particular by those sonnets
challenging time and promising the young man eternal fame
through the poet's 'powerful rhyme.' These promises are a
development of the poet's concern that the young man shall
himself reproduce his beauty by marrying. If he will not beget
a child, the poet will frustrate time in his own creative fashion;
preserving in verse an image of the beauty which the young
man might renew in his own substance. It is in the course of
this proposal that the speaker first reveals, in Sonnet 15, that he
possesses such a creative power; without yet revealing that he
is a poet:

> As he takes from you, I engraft you new.

He refers to his profession more explicitly in all but one of the
six ensuing sonnets, speaking of 'my verse', 'my rhyme', and
modestly of 'my pupil pen.' A long run of poems then substantially ignores the subject; but of the first hundred and twenty
sonnets, thirty-two make some clear allusion to his writing.
These include the bold assertions of creative talent that close
some of the great sonnets on Time,

> My love shall in my verse ever live young
>
> [19

and

> His beauty shall in these black lines be seen;
>
> [63

which do most to uphold the belief that Shakespeare himself
is speaking. The poet's boldness is seen to have been justified:
his work has outlasted tyrants' monuments, and the young
man's beauty lives on as he declared it would. The poetry
which is still read, eternalising a long-dead friend, is incontestably
Shakespeare's; and the implication that he must be the speaker

of the Sonnets generally seems impossible to resist. But two considerations make the position less simple than it appears. If Shakespeare were writing in the character of another poet, he would not deliberately degrade the quality of his verse to make it appear the work of a less gifted man. Other sonnets, in which the poet bemoans the limited scope of his abilities, have endured just as capably despite their supposed mediocrity. The valuation which the poet sets on his work is not always to be taken seriously. This point brings in the second consideration, for most of the speaker's references to his poetry admit a sense of inferiority and incompetence that are incompatible with Shakespeare's admitted greatness among his contemporaries. If nothing were known of the respect which Shakespeare's fellow-poets expressed towards him, there would remain the open disparity between the speaker's depressed admissions of being untalented and ignored, and the superbly confident spirit of his prediction in Sonnet 55,

> Not marble, nor the gilded monuments
> Of princes shall outlive this powerful rhyme.

This is the voice we might expect of Shakespeare, announcing awareness of his creative power in language matching its heroic vigour. Such a gift finds part of its natural idiom in the calmly assured forecast of Sonnet 81,

> Your name from hence immortal life shall have;

which fails in its promise only because it omits to name the friend; and which is implausibly associated with the inadequate being who harps on his discontent,

> Desiring this man's art, and that man's scope.
> [29

The Sonnets could be a work of collaboration between two poets; one proudly grandiloquent though never merely boastful, the other claiming little for himself though not always to be taken at his word when he seems most self-effacing. To suppose that this second speaker is identical with the poet who promises immortality to the friend seems to be ruled out by his own admission that his writing lacks power to impress itself upon time. One might argue that Shakespeare was not always as confident of his power as Sonnet 55 suggests, but the disparity between these two voices raises doubts whether either represents him. The poet presents himself in two distinct characters; and unless the disparity is consciously noticed it may be easy to extend the sense of Shakespearian presence that is so marked in the sonnets on Time to the whole sequence, despite the much quieter tone of most of its poems.

The richly orchestrated writing of these challenges to Time, in which the poet displays the power that will make good his predictions, embodies a creative energy which the narrator of the more intimate sonnets might well envy. This minor poet, who repeatedly laments that his invention has dried up, knows himself overshadowed by rivals who, if not much more gifted, are much less reluctant to advertise themselves. Unable to compete for attention with the flamboyant style which these younger poets have made fashionable, he can only hope to secure a hearing by offering simple compliments whose true affection the friend will recognise. Sonnet 32 describes his writing in typically self-depreciatory terms, 'poor rude lines . . . outstripped by every pen', and asks the friend to

> Reserve them for my love, not for their rhyme,
> Exceeded by the height of happier men.

He acknowledges that his range of expression is sadly limited, and that while other poets experiment with new and exciting modes of writing, he continues 'still all one, ever the same'; repeating himself in the uninspired process of

dressing old words new.
Spending again what is already spent.
[76

This might be accepted as a just comment on the Sonnets'
persistent re-working of a restricted area of experience, but the
poet is not making this point: he complains that his praise of the
young man introduces no fresh form of argument. In fact
he does vary the reasons which he gives for repeating himself.
The friend is 'still constant in a wondrous excellence,' he explains in Sonnet 105; and it follows that his poetry, 'to constancy confined,' shall adopt the same character. He has no new
ideas to express, Sonnet 108 admits, and 'must each day say o'er
the very same'; but the words which he addressed to the friend
at the beginning of their acquaintance remain still fresh, and
are not to be accounted old in repetition. Sonnet 76 offers the
simpler explanation that since the poet has only one unvarying
subject, he has no need to 'glance aside to new-found methods'
which the age thinks fashionable. The worried self-questioning
of the octet,

> Why write I still all one, ever the same,
> And keep invention in a noted weed,
> That every word doth almost tell my name?

gives way to reassurance in the sestet as the poet acknowledges
that his preoccupation with the friend gives him no reason to
change his style, or to devise such 'compounds strange' as
other poets have brought in.

This allusion to contemporary literary style has parallels in
other sonnets, which show a similar indifference or even
hostility towards the kinds of florid and strenuously inventive
writing which the poet finds most alien to his own plain truthfulness. He recognises that his poetry is out-dated and commonplace, but refuses to conform with a vogue for extravagant
compliment whose showiness declares it insincere. In Sonnet 21

he announces his contempt for those who follow so artificial a fashion:

> So is it not with me as with that Muse,
> Stirred by a painted beauty to his verse,
> Who heaven itself for ornament doth use.

This sense of his moral superiority over poets better-esteemed than himself is absent in Sonnet 85, where the speaker stands respectfully tongue-tied while more gifted poets put his own thoughts with much greater refinement and polish:

> comments of your praise richly compiled
> Reserve their character with golden quill,
> And precious phrase by all the Muses filed.[1]

Here the poet compares himself to an 'unlettered clerk' who can only assent with opinions far more ably expressed than his own meagre gifts would allow. There is some possibility that he is already speaking with the irony that colours the more famous sonnet that follows; but the self-depreciation of Sonnet 85 characterises the poet, whether he is referring to his literary abilities or to his qualities as a man. Outside the grandly assured statements of the sonnets on Time, little suggests that the poet supposes his work or himself to possess any virtue beyond simple truth of emotion.

The conflict between this simplicity and the poetry of hyperbolic compliment which he condemns provides the theme of the sonnets on the rival poet, who enters the sequence at Sonnet 79. It does not immediately appear that the rival follows the extravagant fashion already condemned by the poet, who tries to resist his influence by arguing that, although the friend deserves the tribute 'of a worthier pen', when the rival praises him he merely reflects the qualities of beauty and virtue he has found in the friend. In Sonnet 80 he admits his inferiority to the

[1] 'Preserve their style by labouring it precisely'; Onions.

'better spirit' whose more vociferous praises have silenced his own modest utterance;

> I am a worthless boat,
> He of tall building, and of goodly pride.

Here again it is possible to read an ironic purpose into the poet's underlining of his own inadequacy: the humility is a little too deliberate, and his respect for the rival's effortless superiority rather too deferential for these valuations to be taken at face value. Dover Wilson may be right to suppose that the next poem should have followed Sonnet 74; but it seems a happy accident that makes the actual sequel to the self-abasing Sonnet 80 speak out boldly of the poet's greatness. When he returns to the story of the rival in Sonnet 82 the poet is less subdued, and ready to show his spirit by again challenging the other's right to the friend's complete respect. Accepting that the friend cannot be satisfied with his inarticulate praise, the poet encourages him to

> seek anew
> Some fresher stamp of the time-bettering days;

but predicts that the friend will find a truer account of himself in the unpretentious simplicity of writing which shuns the 'gross painting' currently in fashion. 'When they have devised,' he remarks of such poets,

> What strained touches rhetoric can lend,
> Thou, truly fair, wert truly sympathised[1]
> In true plain words, by thy true-telling friend.

Sonnet 105 repeats the argument in a different form. The conception of Shakespeare as a sincere, unaffectedly truthful friend refusing to fall in with a shallow literary mode has proved attractive; though this assumption has the less agreeable corollary that Shakespeare is also the shameful lover of the Dark

[1] sympathised=matched

Lady sonnets. But if we are to regard the poet's remarks about his character as statements applying literally to Shakespeare, we must–to be consistent–also be ready to accept the Sonnets at the valuation which the poet sets upon them. They do not, in fact, tally with the account which he gives of his work. To take a simple instance, the poet who produced the suavely finished line,

And precious phrase by all the Muses filed
[85

clearly did not lack the deftness and elegance of expression which he speaks of envying in his competitors. If we offer the reasonable comment that poetic licence allows Shakespeare to refer to the speaker's awkwardness without himself adopting a clumsy form of speech–as in the plays plebeians may express themselves in blank verse–we have surrendered to the view that Shakespeare is not speaking in his own character. A reader who credits the poet's repeated complaint of being tongue-tied has not studied the Sonnets very attentively.

A more realistic appreciation of the Sonnets discards both this and the notion that the poet expresses himself 'in true plain words', and without recourse to elaborate rhetorical figures and other fashionable literary devices. No Elizabethan poet of consequence wrote by ignoring the disciplines of formal rhetoric; least of all Shakespeare. In their systematic development of idea and argument, as in their patterns of language, the Sonnets reveal a continuous and absorbed concern with literary artifice. If the 'strained touches' of the rival's rhetoric imply a use of bombastic and unnaturally forced images, we may agree that in this respect he and Shakespeare adopt different criteria; but this does not mean that Shakespeare writes as simply as the poet of the Sonnets suggests. The poems on Time, which most clearly refute the speaker's picture of himself as ill-assured and ungifted, employ a boldly rhetorical idiom in keeping with their storming energy and confidence. To assert in the face of such monumental writing that he was 'a worthless boat' daunted by a rival's towering magnificence, the poet must either have his tongue in his cheek or be dissociating himself from the companion figure who makes his poetry a challenge to Time. The language of the Sonnets, generally considered, is certainly not plain; nor are the poet's compliments always as unpretentiously direct as he suggests when he discusses his writing. His praise of the friend in Sonnet 53,

> Describe Adonis, and the counterfeit
> Is poorly counterfeited after you;

or his rebuke to the forward violet in a later poem,

> Sweet thief, whence didst thou steal thy sweet that smells,
> If not from my love's breath?
>
> [99

exemplify the kind of lavish and elaborate personal eulogy that might be written to display virtuosity or to win favour, but not to express simple feeling. In point of style, both poems are condemned by the poet's own censuring of extravagant comparison in Sonnet 21, directed against a rival who 'heaven itself for ornament doth use'. But this poem itself seems equivocal in its condemnation of a poetic practice which the speaker is certainly well-qualified to follow. As he catalogues the rich and exotic similes recited by such poets in praising 'a painted beauty', mockery gives way to a shared sense of wonder, as though the poet were himself yielding to the delight of shaping hyperbolic compliment,

> With April's first-born flowers and all things rare
> That heaven's air in this huge rondure hems.

Although he insists that he is not prepared to praise the friend in such lavish terms, the poet admits himself enraptured by the

69

beauty of natural creation, which he describes in language well above the level of simple plainness. His friend too is beautiful, he grants,

> though not so bright
> As those gold candles fixed in heaven's air.

The comparison implies likeness, despite the poet's ostensible attempt to deny a similarity; and again the exalted tone of his allusion to natural beauty makes his refusal to enthuse over the friend's good looks seem a form of reticence deliberately imposed. The idiom of rhapsodic praise is clearly not uncongenial to the poet. His picture of a majestic sun 'gilding pale streams with heavenly alchemy,' and his reference to the mother who 'calls back the lovely April of her prime' in the friend's beauty, have both a fluency and a richness of expression which–if we credited all the poet's remarks about his style–would surprise us.

His allusions to his outdated manner of writing could be equally misleading. When he admits that his friend must feel dissatisfied with such inadequate tributes, and look elsewhere for more gifted poetry–'some fresher stamp of the time-bettering days'–the poet suggests that changes in literary fashion have left him behind. There may be an earlier hint of his standing apart from contemporary trends of poetry in Sonnet 38, where although the tone of his remark

> If my slight Muse do please these curious days

suggests a certain ironic reserve, the poet speaks as though he expects his modest achievement to be ignored. His plainest admission of having failed to keep abreast of modish innovation comes in Sonnet 76, where the poet asks himself why he does not conform with current practice by adopting 'new-found methods' and 'compounds strange.' If the second reference is to compound epithets, his question can hardly be serious;

for such terms appear throughout the sequence: all-eating, all-oblivious, all-tyrant, blessed-fair, dear-purchased, ever-fixed, fore-bemoaned, frantic-mad, heart-inflaming, master-mistress, ill-wresting, never-resting, pity-wanting, proud-pied, self-substantial, swart-complexioned, time-bettering, true-telling, wilful-slow and world-without-end. In the narrative poems compounds of this kind are still more numerous,[1] and the device is clearly a prominent feature of Shakespeare's early style. When the poet of Sonnet 76 asks why he does not sub-scribe to this stylistic fashion he cannot be writing in Shakes-peare's character. The question might be an almost explicit indication to the reader of the Sonnets that the supposed speaker of this poem is a persona assumed by Shakespeare, and pointedly unlike him. The circle of friends who first saw the Sonnets, and who knew Shakespeare's standing among the poets of his day, could not have supposed him to be speaking of himself. Perhaps the best means of refuting the possibility that Shakespeare could have been serious when he wrote as a poet outdated and eclipsed during this productive opening phase of his career, is to compare his work with the attempts of other Elizabethan poets to master the same wittily inventive style. What in them is laboured, in him is instinctive and effortless. The wit and inventiveness which Shakespeare was about to display in the narrative poems were already attracting attention in 1592, when Chettle spoke of the poet's 'facetious grace in writing'; and the early plays demonstrated these abilities in still more striking manner. In the field in which most Elizabethan poets of note before Jonson wished to distinguish themselves, Shakespeare was the outstanding figure; as the

[1] *E.g.,* all-hiding, cloud-kissing, dead-killing, ever-during, feast-finding, feeling-painful, hard-believing, heavy-hanging, key-cold, life-poisoning, night-wandering, pity-pleading, poor-rich, quick-shifting, self-slaughtered, sick-thoughted, silly-mild, still-gazing, time-beguiling, true-sweet, weak-built, wreck-threatening, wrinkled-old.

Sonnets themselves help to show in the versatility of their wit.
Modern taste does not care for verbal ingenuity, whether it
juggles expertly with different senses of the same word—

> How would thy shadow's form form happy show?
>
> [43

uses alliteration as a decorative figure,

> But day doth daily draw my sorrows longer,
>
> [28

or doubles word-sounds in phrases whose plain sense is confused by their noise; as in 'when first your eye I eyed.' What
most modern readers condemn as a trivial mannerism, Elizabethans were ready to accept as proof of inventive ability; which
was for them an immediate criterion of the talent which surpasses nature in her own characteristic activity. The speaker
of the Sonnets who complains of his 'blunt invention,' who
admits that his writing is repetitive and unvaried, and that he is
confined to a single subject, is a poet whose limitations would
have appeared still more disabling in Elizabethan eyes than
modern readers may appreciate. To believe that Shakespeare
could have uttered such complaints on his own behalf might
be possible if his apologies for drab and monotonous writing
were borne out in the Sonnets; but the reverse is true.

When he speaks of himself, the poet continues to be apologetic and self-depreciating. Very little emerges with any
definiteness. He makes no attempt to fill in the background of
his commentary, and does not refer to any specific places or to
the setting of events. It might be interesting to know where, if
at all, the poet saw morning flatter mountain-tops, and waves
making towards a pebbled shore. Of his references to his own
condition, perhaps the clearest are those alluding to his lack of
youth. The advice to marry and have children seems to be
offered by an adviser older than the young man; and in Sonnet

22 the poet reveals the disparity of years between himself and the friend by trying to conceal it in a conceit:

How can I then be elder than thou art?

Sonnet 37 implies that the poet is considerably older than his friend, who stands in the relation of 'active child' to the poet, his 'decrepit father.' The comparison is evidently playful, but consistent with other suggestions of the poet's seniority. In Sonnet 62 these are particularised by an unexpectedly graphic image of the face reflected by the poet's mirror,

Beaten and chopped with tanned antiquity.

The image remains with the poet in the next sonnet, in which he contemplates the time when his friend will have reached the same wretched state as himself;

With Time's injurious hand crushed and o'erworn.
[63

Old age takes a long step towards the poet in Sonnet 73, where he describes himself in terms of a wintry bough, a dying fire, and a day about to be swallowed by night; and warns the friend that he must expect to be parted from him soon. He may still be able to satisfy a mistress, however; though to keep relations even between them each must credit the other's lie, the mistress pretending

that she thinks me young,
Although she knows my days are past the best.
[138

This modifies the picture of 'tanned antiquity' which the poet presents as a self-portrait earlier in the sequence, but still calls for a factual corrective. Shakespeare reached the age of thirty in 1596, when many of the sonnets had probably been written. It is a reasonable assumption that when Sonnets 138 and 144 were published in 1599 the sequence was complete; for the latter of them reads like a commentary on the whole matter of the Sonnets. The furthest likelihood, then, is that Shakespeare was at most thirty-three when he wrote the last of the sonnets, and appreciably younger when he began the series. Elizabethans, we may be reminded, aged more rapidly than ourselves; but if Shakespeare was indeed as time-worn in his early thirties as some of the poet's allusions imply, it might be difficult to explain how he contrived to live for another twenty years. As a dramatist, Shakespeare's creative maturity began with the new century. His energies as a poet had not revealed themselves fully when Meres made the famous reference to Shakespeare's 'sugred sonnets'; and he was hardly to be described as 'crushed and outworn' when he was about to enter the phase of his greatest achievements. To interpret the remark literally would be absurdly credulous. Either Shakespeare is speaking facetiously, exaggerating a modest difference in years and condition, or he is giving a voice to the unimposing counterpart who tells the story of the Sonnets and presents its poems as his own. Even without the knowledge that Shakespeare was much younger than the lined and wasted figure whom the Sonnets describe, we might suspect him of arranging an antithesis between the friend's youthful beauty and the aged and disfigured poet. Such an antithesis is nascent from the beginning of the sequence, in the poet's warnings that Time will ravage the friend's good looks,

> besiege thy brow,
> And dig deep trenches in thy beauty's field.
> [2

It persists in the related image of Sonnet 60, where Time 'delves the parallels in beauty's brow'; and assumes an oddly equivocal form in the opening remarks of Sonnet 68:

> Thus is his cheek the map of days outworn.

74

The poet means that the friend's face reveals the beauty of a bygone age, before true appearances were disguised by 'bastard signs of fair'; but at first reading 'outworn' seems to qualify 'map of days', and to suggest that the friend personifies old age. This impression remains when the complimentary sense of the phrase is recognised; and the reader may then feel that the friend appears in a double aspect, both as his youthful self and as the 'outworn' figure to which he is reduced. He is then his own antithesis. To make the poet embody the state of 'crushed and outworn age' which offsets the friend's unmarked beauty is a more obvious means of exploiting the same antithetical figure.

Whether we take the speaker to be Shakespeare or not, the inconsistency and sometimes the improbability of his allusions to his age should make us wary of giving literal regard to his remarks about his personal circumstances. Because the poet's comments are so indefinite, they can very easily be made to corroborate interpretations which begin by assuming that the Sonnets contain allusions to Shakespeare's personal and professional life. Although the speaker never claims any connection with the playhouse, critics continue to find references to his association with acting and drama in every sonnet which hints at the poet's means of livelihood. To any dispassionate scrutiny such imparticular allusions reveal nothing, and their very indefiniteness invites the reader to make of them whatever he likes. In the absence of any clear directive, it is better to fall back upon the critical axiom that the poems themselves lay down the terms on which they are to be understood, and not to expect the circumstances of Shakespeare's life to explain them. Instead of assuming that the speaker's allusions to his background can only refer to Shakespeare's social status and professional career, we should question all such remarks very closely; seeking to understand them primarily within the context of ideas which the sequence develops, and of which they form part.

It begins to appear early in the sequence that the poet is dogged by misfortune, which conspires with other disabilities to thwart his hopes. Others, better favoured than himself, may boast of 'public honours and proud titles': he is denied such happiness, and must draw a compensating pleasure from the friendship which he has found unlooked-for [25]. In describing himself as one 'whom fortune of such triumph bars', the poet does not explain what prevents him from becoming distinguished; but those who read the Sonnets as autobiography recognise here the first of several allusions to the stigma which Shakespeare incurred by following the calling of common player. A more sceptical reader may suspect that the poet inflicts this arbitrary disqualification upon himself for the sake of antithesis with those who are 'in favour with their stars.' The argument of the sonnet invites such a playing of one against the other. Those who have secured a place in the public eye are not to be envied, for they may suddenly lose it; whereas the poet, although unknown and ungifted, enjoys the happiness of a mutual love too firm ever to be lost. There is no critical justification for putting any more particular construction on the 'public honours and proud titles' which an unkind fate denies the speaker. Shakespeare's status as an actor may have debarred him from certain privileges, though it is not altogether clear what deprivation he suffered as a member of the acting company which, in Chambers' words, 'had practically become an official part of the royal household with a privileged and remunerative position';[1] but he could not well have complained, as the poet does here, that he was unknown and disregarded. The remark becomes intelligible only if we suppose the speaker to be adopting his habitual character of minor poet whose unadventurous verse makes no impression on fashionable taste; though this is not one of the sonnets in which the speaker refers to himself as a poet. Nor is it—*pace*

[1] *William Shakespeare, A Study of Facts and Problems,* Oxford 1930; i. 67-8.

Dowden, whose 'penetrating note' Dover Wilson quotes with approval–the sonnet in which 'Shakespeare makes his first complaint . . . against his low condition.' The speaker nowhere mentions his social standing.

Four sonnets later his personal difficulties have become more acute. The poet now speaks of himself 'in disgrace with fortune and men's eyes', an aggravated form of the distress alluded to previously. The second line,

> I all alone beweep my outcast state,
> [29

offers the convinced more evidence of the stigma attached to Shakespeare's calling; but the ideas of this poem are shaped by its formal structure, which like Sonnet 25 is directed by anti-thesis. When the poet describes himself 'with what I most enjoy contented least', he does not invite us to take him quite literally, but to admire the neatness of his reversed figure. The whole sonnet is organised on the same principle; and in this respect as in its vague suggestion of personal misfortune the poem represents a stronger version of Sonnet 25. The octet is taken up with the poet's account of the frustrations that make him curse his fate:

> Wishing me like to one more rich in hope,
> Featured like him, like him with friends possessed;
> Desiring this man's art, and that man's scope.
> [29

The third of these lines contains the speaker's first admission of his lameness as a writer. Those whose art and scope he envies here are presumably related, in the development of Shakespeare's ideas, with those who have acquired public honour and proud titles in the earlier sonnet; and thus the germinal concept to be seen full-grown in Sonnets 79–86 has been implanted in the sequence. By balancing 'this man's art' against 'that man's

77

scope', and reversing the form of 'featured like him' in a matching phrase, the poet continues to show the concern with antithesis which gives the sonnet its shape. With the opening of the
sestet he reaches the turning-point of the rhetorical figure on
which the poem is organised;

> Yet in these thoughts myself almost despising,
> Haply I think on thee;

and the image of a lark 'at break of day arising' epitomises the
poet's sudden exhilaration of spirit as he recalls the friendship
which outweighs all his discontent. In Sonnet 37 the poet returns
to the same theme, which is simply put after the opening
simile about a decrepit father and his active child:

> So I, made lame by fortune's dearest spite,
> Take all my comfort of thy worth and truth.

The speaker's allusion to his lameness has evoked critical
speculation since Capell took the term in its most literal sense.
The particularity of 'dearest spite' suggests that the poet is
referring to a specific misfortune; and it is a reasonable inference that since he finds comfort in associating himself with
the friend's 'beauty, birth, or wealth, or wit,' the bitter
injury inflicted on him is the lack of these social and intellectual
advantages, which makes him 'lame, poor [and] despised.'
Yet this reading arouses some doubts, which deepen when the
statement is held to concern Shakespeare. Whether he lacked
beauty is an open question, though the Droeshout portrait
does not suggest that he was unhandsome. As to birth, it is
relevant to remember that a grant of arms made Shakespeare a
gentleman in 1596; and still more important to recognise that
it is nowhere clearly stated in the Sonnets that the friend was of
noble blood. Nothing obliges us to believe that the actual
Shakespeare and the anonymous friend of the sequence are
widely separated by social degree. Again, Shakespeare may

not have enjoyed great wealth; but the poet who bought New Place in 1597 – when he was writing sonnets – was not by common standards a poor man. These are objections to be put forward tentatively, conceding that Shakespeare may have been ill-favoured and relatively poor and base; but the complaint that 'fortune's dearest spite' included depriving him of wit makes it impossible to proceed with this reading of the sonnet. Here, as in later poems which take this complaint as their main theme, the speaker describes himself as a poet of meagre gifts and feeble inventive power, and provides the clearest warning that he is not to be mistaken for Shakespeare.

However, the speaker is at least consistent in his complaints. He suffers under an inauspicious star, which frustrates his wish to achieve public fame and respect [25]. He is depressed by fortune and of no consequence in the world at large, and envious of others who enjoy the gifts and personal attractions denied to him [29]. He has been victimised by fate, and is exposed to poverty and contempt [37]. Although Shakespeare cannot be describing his own circumstances, the three poems agree largely over the indistinct figure who finds compensation in the friend's love [25, 29] or outstanding personal qualities [37] for the misfortune and deprivation which he suffers. The three images are not identical, for each account of the poet's ill-starred condition is a new variation on their common theme; and 'fortune's dearest spite' does not indicate a new and more galling injury, but a more forceful variant of the always generalised hardship which the speaker must bear. The fact that he refers to the unkindness of fate only as prelude to describing how the friend transforms his outlook is suggestive. The human antithesis between poet and friend – one young and handsome, the other aged and disfigured; the friend wealthy and accomplished where the poet lacks all claim to respect – is not a fixed condition of the story, but a figure brought in to accompany the antithetical structure of certain sonnets. The standing of the poet is depressed to the point where his sudden change of spirits will be most dramatic, and a striking demonstration of the power of the friend's beauty.

These three poems have an echo later in the sequence, when the poet suspects that the friend is about to abandon him, and begs him not to delay the blow which he may be planning:

> Now while the world is bent my deeds to cross,
> Join with the spite of fortune; make me bow,
> And do not drop in for an after-loss.
>
> [90

Beeching thought that Shakespeare might be referring to the difficulties which his company encountered during the popularity of the 'little eyases' whom Hamlet speaks of; but the sonnet plainly refers to some private trouble which has newly arisen. The hint is not embellished. The family resemblance between 'the spite of fortune' here and 'fortune's dearest spite' in Sonnet 37 suggests that Shakespeare has returned to the theme of interest which provided related references in Sonnet 25 and 29; but the four sonnets are alike in throwing no light on the issue. A final allusion to the speaker's malign fortune in Sonnet 111 deserves to be taken into consideration with this scattered group of poems; for here the poet speaks at greater length and with some seeming particularity about the disadvantages which lame him. He begins by asking the friend to rebuke fortune,

> The guilty goddess of my harmful deeds,
> That did not better for my life provide
> Than public means, which public manners breeds.
> Thence comes it that my name receives a brand;
> And, almost, thence my nature is subdued
> To what it works in, like the dyer's hand.

With Sonnet 110, this poem has provided a happy hunting-ground for those who read Shakespeare into every line of the Sonnets. From Malone in 1780, followed by Dyce who saw these lines as a protest against 'the degradation that accompanies the profession of the stage', few editors or commentators have been able to resist their insinuations; though as early as 1821 Boswell exposed the baselessness of an autobiographical reading by asking;

> Is there anything in these words which, read without a pre-conceived hypothesis, would particularly apply to the publick profession of a player or writer for the stage?[1]

The question answers itself. Neither here nor in any other sonnet does the speaker describe himself as a dramatist or associate himself with the stage. He presents himself as a poet whose writing is confined to lyrical and complimentary verses; and while throughout much of the sequence he addresses his work exclusively to the friend, during the group of sonnets immediately preceding the two poems in question the speaker repeatedly apologises for having neglected this duty. In Sonnet 100 the line, 'Darkening thy power to lend base subjects light', implies that the poet has been courting favour elsewhere: a notion to which Shakespeare seem to returns in the 'worse essays' of Sonnet 110, where the speaker admits having 'sold cheap what is most dear.' If it is right to see a common theme threading these poems together, we shall understand the puzzling allusions of Sonnet 111 better by seeing it as an extension of the poet's apology. Evidently he has been eulogising public figures who do not deserve the praise he has lavished on them in the hope of reward; and thus he has not only denied the friend his proper tribute, but has impugned his own reputation for truth and integrity. Like other episodes in the poet's story, this happening is not described clearly and consistently throughout the group of sonnets concerned, but emerges from the

[1] *Plays and Poems of William Shakespeare,* London 1821. xx.219.

shifting hints of such an occurrence which they contain; and is finally presented as an event which has taken place, and which the poet can allude to as a subject already familiar to his reader. In Sonnet 111 his purpose is to explain to the friend not what he has done, but what circumstances induced him to behave so badly. Fortune is responsible, he argues; for the goddess

> did not better for my life provide
> Than public means, which public manners breeds.

Because she did not favour the poet in his birth, he has had to find a profession and work for his living. The phrase 'public means' does not necessarily imply that the speaker earns his living by making a physical display of himself: he is more likely to be saying that, unlike the nobleman whom he may be addressing, he has no private means and so must earn his livelihood. For the poet, this can come only through patronage; and the temptation to flatter his way into a great man's graces has bred the 'public manners'—the vulgar and undignified pursuit of favour—for which he is now trying to make amends. The remark that follows,

> Thence comes it that my name receives a brand

is of course part of the self-humiliation through which the poet apologises, rather than a statement of fact: he has brought a slur upon his reputation as a true-telling friend, and cannot forgive himself. He has drawn back in time from a dangerous occupation, his nature almost 'subdued to what it works in', but before the habit of flattering insincerity has become too deeply ingrained to be shaken off. Against his 'strong infection' he is willing to accept whatever harsh medicine the friend prescribes.

To read this poem as Shakespeare's lament over his shameful association with the stage requires some determination. The greatest writing in our literature was not produced by a poet ashamed of being a dramatist, but by a man whose superlative gift found its fullest expression in supplying the needs of the most distinguished acting company of his age. Nothing suggests that his work brought him into disgrace. To the contrary, we know that it gave him popularity, modest affluence and contemporary fame which the ill-starred poet of the Sonnets does not hope to achieve. If there were reason to suppose that some body of Elizabethan readers or *cognoscenti* held Shakespeare in contempt for his association with the playhouse, the poem might be read in this sense; but evidently it and Sonnet 110 together provide the whole basis of the assumption. A critic who supposes that Shakespeare is speaking must believe that the poet had just dissociated himself from the stage in disgust and self-reproach, and that in Sonnet 111 he is asking the friend to devise a ritual of purification after his exposure to the mob. We need only ask when this sudden abandonment of the playhouse and his fellow-sharers occurred to reveal the absurdity of a reading which makes Shakespeare its speaker.

Sonnet 110 seems to encourage this reading by using the term 'motley', which most critics have taken in a theatrical sense. A more detached appreciation of the poem will recognise another admission of the inconstancy for which the speaker had already rebuked himself in Sonnet 100, coupled with an assurance that he has profited by his mistake, and a plea for a renewal of the friend's affection. Here again the notion that Shakespeare is admitting what shame he has incurred by joining the Lord Chamberlain's Men does not match the terms of the experience outlined in the sonnet; for unlike the speaker, Shakespeare did not–if he discovered that he had committed himself to an ignominious course of life–withdraw from it in disgust. The opening lines of the poem leave us in no doubt of the poet's self-contemptuous feelings:

Alas, 'tis true, I have gone here and there,
And made myself a motley to the view;
Gored mine own thoughts, sold cheap what is most dear,
Made old offences of affections new.
Most true it is that I have looked on truth
Askance and strangely.

His mortification seems centred upon the recognition that he has acted without respect for the truth which the friend embodies, and which his own writing has hitherto reflected. Previously the poet has been able to claim an honest sincerity for his writing which made amends for its lack of fashionable polish: the friend might value him for this simple truth of feeling, although other poets put him to shame by their greater fluency and eloquence. Sonnet 100 marks a change of behaviour, whose consequences are indicated or hinted at in two groups of poems which follow. The first group deals with the poet's silence towards the friend, and offers the various explanations compared in Chapter 2 above. These include a suggestion that the poet has found a new and less distinguished patron, on whom he has been squandering his talent. This idea lies dormant until Sonnet 109, which opens a group of poems apologising and begging forgiveness for an act never clearly defined, but which is half-identified with the suggested disloyalty of Sonnet 100. The poems of this group, Sonnets 109–112, develop a situation seemingly drawn from this idea thrown out earlier; and present a state of affairs appreciably more serious than the previous group of sonnets outlines, though still related to it. Both show the poet on the defensive, and trying to persuade either himself or the friend that his love is unaffected by the aberrations of behaviour that have plainly indicated a weakening of regard for the friend. This is the background of 'story' against which Sonnets 109–112 are to be read.

'Alas, 'tis true', is part of the aftermath of the poet's

negligence and disloyalty. He has betrayed the standards that
made him unselfishly constant despite the friend's ill-treatment.
Still more astonishing, the friend has undergone as complete a
metamorphosis. He is now – and to judge from the terms of the
poet's self-reproach, has always been – as staunch in affection as
the poet was earlier: 'a god in love.' The poet confesses shame
at having neglected such a proved friendship for the sake of
general esteem, won at the cost of his personal reputation for
loyalty.[1] His fickleness has been noted. His next remark,
'Gored mine own thoughts', appears to renew this admission;
'thoughts' being the good opinion in which he had previously
been held, and which he himself has injured. It is not an
isolated lapse for which he condemns himself: 'Made old
offences of affections new' admits that he has persisted in his
fault and become habituated to inconstancy. Most true it is, he
continues with an ironic play on words, that he has wrenched
himself away from the well-tried truth of the friend, to whom
he now appeals abjectly for pardon. The reading of Sonnet 110
followed by the autobiographists, who take 'motley' as a
keyword referring to Shakespeare's professional life, fails to
offer any coherent explanation of the poet's self-accusing
remarks. As Tucker observed, in following his profession an
actor does not gore his own thoughts, and still less can he be
said to 'make old offences of affections new.'

The poet renews his apology and his appeal in Sonnet 117;
an unexpected sequel to the fine poem on 'the marriage of true
minds', which although not referring to the friend, suggests
that their shaken relationship has been stabilised. Perhaps Sonnet 117 should stand with the previous group of poems, for its
self-condemnation

---

[1] The denigrating term 'motley' has the now obsolete sense of varying in
character or mood: see *OED motley* 3, and compare Donne, Satire 1:
'Away, thou changeling motley humorist.'

that I have scanted all
Wherein I should your great deserts repay,

is closely related in manner to the speaker's listing of his faults
in Sonnet 110; but its position suggests rather that Shakespeare
revived this theme a little later. The second half of the octet
contains a clear indictment of the wrongs done to the poet by
his friend, and fills out the previously incomplete picture of the
'harmful deeds' mentioned but not specified in Sonnet 111:

> That I have frequent been with unknown minds,
> And given to time your own dear-purchased right;
> That I have hoisted sail to all the winds
> Which should transport me farthest from your sight.

With the figurative expression of hoisting sail the accusations
begin to yield to the indefiniteness which has promoted such
oddly literal readings of other sonnets; and one almost expects
to see these lines adduced as evidence that Shakespeare made a
voyage overseas, callously ignoring his obligation to a noble
patron. Whether in plain or figurative language, familiar
accusations are being repeated as Shakespeare continues to work
and reshape the limited material he has elected to make his
subject. The speaker has repaid his friend's kindness with
negligence and deliberate disregard; deserting the friend at
every opportunity, and slighting his constant affection by
spending his time in other company, where he has squandered
the friend's rights in him. The 'unknown minds' with whom
the poet has been intimate have appeared before; in the 'base
subjects' of Sonnet 100, and by inference in the shallow associates who have encouraged the poet to make himself a motley.
The persistence of these ideas, and the renewal of the poet's
appeal through a new explanation of his motives, shows this
poem to be another variation on the theme developed earlier;
and invites us to use it as a means of elucidating the more
puzzling features of Sonnets 109–112. As there is no reference

to actual events in these poems, we cannot expect to tie down their meaning very firmly; and if Shakespeare is writing variations on a theme which is itself not entirely constant, there will be still less reason for expecting a single, definite picture to emerge from this group of sonnets. But they treat a kindred subject, and in Sonnet 117 Shakespeare seems to have revealed more clearly the kind of situation to which all five poems refer. Here, in speaking more plainly about his disloyalty and unkindness, the poet makes it much harder to suppose that he is expressing shame about his life as a common player; for none of his expressions contain any certain allusion to the stage. By regarding this poem as the key to the controversial subject behind the earlier apologies, rather than as a postscript to the series, we may reach a truer appreciation of the character in which Shakespeare is presenting his speaker.

This figure appears in two main aspects. In his earlier personal allusions, the speaker describes himself as a man unkindly treated by fortune, which has denied him the advantages showered on the friend. To offset and outweigh these disabling circumstances, he has the friend's intimate companionship, which makes amends even for the meagreness of his poetic talent. His complaint against fortune is echoed in the later group of sonnets, where the speaker tries to shift the blame for his shabby behaviour from himself to the fate that made him dependent upon patronage; but this link with his earlier attitude is not maintained. The speaker now appears predominantly as a man who has betrayed a close friendship, either wilfully or because he saw easy popularity and acclaim offered him elsewhere. From the self-pitying postures of his complaints against fortune, cancelled when he recalls the happiness of his intimacy with the friend, the poet moves later in the sequence to self-accusation and apology; blaming himself for his misconduct and trying earnestly to repair the trust he has damaged. There is no likelihood that Shakespeare himself voiced such complaints against the fortune that obliged him to find his living as sharer in the leading dramatic company of his age; and nothing associates him with the speaker's self-accusing admissions of having 'gone here and there' in an undignified search for favour and quick returns. If these sonnets have some special application to Shakespeare, their significance is more likely to lie in the fuller understanding of human character which they disclose. The speaker who is at first content to blame the stars for his personal shortcomings comes to know himself better, and recognises impulses within himself entirely alien to the rational being he has hitherto supposed himself to be. In a final group of sonnets forming a sequel to the poet's self-injuring perversity, the speaker makes a horrified acknowledgement of the idiot purposes that have assumed control of him:

> What wretched errors hath my heart committed
> Whilst it hath thought itself so blessed never?
> How have mine eyes out of their spheres been fitted
> In the distraction of this madding fever?
>
> [119

At this point of the sequence the sonnets begin to reflect an awareness of man's divided nature not even faintly adumbrated in its opening phase. The poet begins by regarding the friend as an embodiment of beauty and truth, and comes by degrees to perceive that charm and good looks have misled him. Where the poet becomes aware of moral hypocrisy in the friend, the story changes direction: the friend regains the integrity which has previously been impugned, and is injured by the poet to whom his weaknesses are transferred. This exchange of roles allows the speaker to examine from within the kind of vicious impulse which, in the friend, he knew only from the outside; and to bring himself imaginatively to terms with the nature of the impulsive being which acts in man independently of his moral consciousness, and in defiance of it. Such an awareness

88

seems not to have come within reach of the younger Shakespeare, who gave his speaker a grudge against fortune, but no disposition to look into his private weaknesses. This sharper appreciation of man's hidden self appears to have been acquired during the writing of the Sonnets, which are in this respect a record of the development of Shakespeare's moral outlook. After the two linked poems in which the speaker tries to understand what perverse impulse induced him to act against all better counsel and inclination, the relationship of poet and friend seems to have offered Shakespeare no further means of pursuing an imaginatively dominant theme. The story could only be continued through some basic change of circumstance which involved the narrator in a different form of personal relationship; and accordingly with Sonnet 127 a new and unlovely friend enters the story.

CHAPTER FOUR

The Dark Lady

THE shorter sequence which begins with Sonnet 127 comprises twenty-eight poems. Of these the two last are the alternative versions of a legend about a hot spring, and one is a poem in octosyllabic lines which shares no common ground with the remaining twenty-five sonnets. These carry forward the story of the narrator's emotional life by describing his association – liaison might be too positive a term – with a woman for whom the Dark Lady is an accepted and convenient title. This form of reference is not always appropriate, for the degree of emphasis which falls upon the lady's colour varies a good deal, and it does not always appear that she is black in either sense of the word. Six sonnets describe her unequivocally as black; one asserts that she is 'coloured ill', and another refers to her foul face. Most of the speaker's comments on her looks suggest, generally with some force, that she is ill-favoured. 'Some say that thee behold,' he tells her bluntly in Sonnet 131,

> Thy face hath not the power to make love groan;

and later he denies that her appearance holds any charm for him: his heart perversely dotes on her 'despite of view.' On the other hand, in Sonnet 139 he speaks of her 'pretty looks'; and although the phrase is not to be understood entirely in its modern sense,[1] it must imply some measure of personal attractiveness. Sonnet 127 takes this complimentary purpose appreciably further, by telling the lady that her black eyes become her so well

> That every tongue says beauty should look so.

[1] 'Fetching glances' might be the present-day equivalent.

But ten sonnets make no allusion to her appearance, whether good or bad; and it may be open to question whether the speaker is addressing the same woman throughout. The disjointed nature of the story of their relationship could be held to show that more than one woman is involved; or better, that the conception of a particular Dark Lady was not in Shakespeare's mind from the outset.

The sonnets of the Dark Lady sequence are widely varied in tone and matter, to an extent which makes it difficult to believe that they are arranged as Shakespeare wrote them. The angry attack on lust in Sonnet 129, for instance, stands between an entirely playful address to a lady at the keyboard and a satirical inversion of Petrarchan attitudes in 'My mistress eyes are nothing like the sun'; dissociated from them as widely as they from each other. The three sonnets 143–5 are similarly disconnected. The first, 'Lo, as a careful housewife', describes the mistress pursuing a man who disdains her, and being in turn pursued by her 'poor infant'–the neglected lover who tells the story. Next comes the crucial sonnet, 'Two loves I have': an account of the conflicting influences of 'a man right fair' and the dark female spirit which seeks to tempt this better angel from him. The sequel in Sonnet 145 is a pretty poem in octosyllabics about a mistress who is gentle and merciful./As there is no certainty that Shakespeare wrote the sonnets of this tailpiece in a narrative order, a new arrangement of the poems which produces a more consequent story does not necessarily restore a quality which they lost through careless handling of the manuscript. If Shakespeare's purpose was not to tell a story but to contrive variations on certain mainly Petrarchan themes, he would have paid very little attention to the story-line which most critics expect him to follow. By giving the sonnets of this sequence even less of a narrative thread than those involving the young man, Shakespeare suggests that he is now more completely absorbed in the ideas which the narrative situations allow him to work out and develop. The Petrarchan figures form only a point of departure for an imaginative exploration of the increasingly confused state of being which the lover undergoes, as he recognises both the moral worthlessness of the lady and his powerlessness to resist her hateful attraction. If there is a case for arranging these poems in a different order, it would have the object of clarifying the development of the lover's self-awareness. Setting the sonnets in groups determined by the extent of the speaker's respect for the lady and the sharpness of his moral perception, we may distinguish five phases of relationship; or alternatively, five increasingly satirical variations on themes of Petrarchan love.

Group (i) is characterised by the first poem of the sequence, Sonnet 127. The lover is uncritically adoring towards a mistress who, although unfashionably dark, is quite certainly beautiful. To defend his judgement, he argues ingeniously that since true beauty has been discredited by the widespread use of cosmetics, black has inherited the title and become the standard of beauty. His allusion to artifice,

> Fairing the foul with art's false borrowed face,

gives a new twist to ideas familiar from the main sequence, and hints forward to the harshly outspoken comments on the lady's foulness in later sonnets. For the moment, however, she stands above reproach in looks as in moral character: her eyes, 'raven black', mourning over the debasement of beauty by those who compensate for the lack of natural good looks by counterfeiting;

> Slandering creation with a false esteem.

In this sadness, her eyes assume a still greater attraction, and she is acclaimed despite her blackness as a pattern for all beautiful women: 'every tongue says beauty should look so.' This reverential attitude towards the mistress is reversed so sharply in the later poems of the sequence that we may feel encouraged to look more closely into the speaker's compliments here, where vocabulary if not idiom suggests an intention at odds with rapturous praise. The poem leaves its reader to recognise in 'fairing the foul with art's false borrowed face' an acknowledgement that the speaker is himself doing exactly that–using rhetorical ingenuity to prove black fair, and ugliness attractive. The perversity of his argument foreshadows his behaviour later in the relationship, when he admits how absurdly misguided his passion is, but is helpless to correct himself. The veiled equivocations of this poem are echoed in Sonnet 132, which is closely related in idea and attitude.[1] Here again the lady's eyes 'have put on black' to present themselves as loving mourners; and again the lover finds the effect ravishing, and is moved to tell the lady that, truly,

> not the morning sun of heaven
> Better becomes the grey cheeks of the east,
> Nor that full star that ushers in the even
> Doth half that glory to the sober west
> As those two mourning eyes become thy face.

Their grief is now differently explained: knowing that their mistress torments the lover with her disdainful heart, they have gone into mourning for pity of his plight. Since this colour becomes her so well, he argues, she should let her heart too mourn for him, and adopt this mark of pity generally:

> Then will I swear beauty herself is black,
> And all they foul that thy complexion lack.

Doubts about the purpose of this sonnet begin with its lavish similes; not for their extravagance alone, but for their apparently

[1] It will be seen from this that I do not accept the arrangement proposed by Brents Stirling, in which these two sonnets stand sixth and twelfth respectively.

deliberate ineptness. Black eyes can hardly glorify the lady's face in the way the sun or the evening star give lustre to the sky. The confusion of bright with dark seems wanton; as though the speaker either wished to express his contempt for the lady under cover of an over-generous compliment or—more probably—was betraying the foolishly deranged state of mind which she has induced in him. The second impression is supported by his readiness in the couplet to 'swear beauty herself is black'; a promise which reveals the full extent of his infatuation. In the happiness of her surrender he will be prepared to deny the most obvious truth, and to stand common judgement on its head by swearing that to be fair is to be ugly. The absurdity of such an argument raises the question whether the lady is in fact as beautiful as the lover invites us to suppose. By playing on the two senses of 'fair', both sonnets repeatedly make the association of blonde with beauty and black with ugliness which the speaker is trying to disprove: but in proposing cross-associations —'beauty herself is black'—he makes nonsense of the terms which his argument employs; for the beautiful and the fair are synonymous. Unlike the poet of the first sequence, who begins by seeking increase 'of fairest creatures', the lover of the Dark Lady is in pursuit of a creature who is admittedly not fair in complexion, and who is to be seen as fair in the second sense only if the speaker's paradoxical standards are accepted.

These two linked sonnets provide a starting-point from which the rest of the sequence is developed stage by stage. In his plaintive but undemanding adoration, the lover is as typically Petrarchan a figure as the disdainful mistress whom he addresses. He appeals only for pity, and appears to have no more thought of making the lady his mistress in a more positive sense than she has inclination to surrender herself to him. So far the reader is on familiar ground; but the blank announce-ment that the lady is black, and the implicit disclosure of wanton absurdity in the lover, warn him that Shakespeare does not intend merely to renew traditional attitudes. The lover may have persuaded himself that his mistress is beautiful despite her damning colour; but by wilfully blinding himself to the truth he is discrediting both his protestations and the conventions of courtship which poetry had substituted for the realities of man's sexual behaviour.

In the sonnets of group (ii) the speaker discards some of his illusions, though without entirely abandoning the attitudes of Petrarchan devotion. He has now come to terms with the fact of the lady's unattractive appearance; but despite this awareness he remains enslaved by her, and she continues to treat him with cruel contempt for his feelings. In his resentment he can speak bluntly of her unkindness, and even taunt her with her want of the beauty that might justify pride:

> Thou art as tyrannous, so as thou art,
> As those whose beauties proudly make them cruel;

he tells her in Sonnet 131; but then admits that he himself encourages this cruelty by the perverse impulse that values her at a rate far beyond her true worth:

> For well thou know'st, to my dear doting heart
> Thou art the fairest and most precious jewel.

The ambivalence which Sonnet 132 hints at is now clearly recognised by the speaker, who knows himself irresistibly drawn by a woman whose defects are as obvious to him as to the on-looker who sees nothing attractive about her. To assure himself that this report is unjust, he groans a thousand times 'but thinking on thy face'; responding, it might seem, both to her personal fascination and to his awareness that she is ugly; but the compliment is forced. The comment which sums up his attitude to the lady,

> Thy black is fairest in my judgement's place

shows the same divided purpose as before, and the same

readiness to invert the sense of words to satisfy a perverse judgement. The next line sets right the false impression which the speaker has just given. The mistress remains ill-favoured, but not because her colour is unfashionable:

> In nothing art thou black save in thy deeds.

This introduces a new idea, for the moment indistinct, which later sonnets will enlarge upon. The poems of group (ii) keep this hint of the lady's misdeeds in the background, as though unwilling to press the point; or as though the speaker's exasperated feelings have not yet goaded him into disclosing his mistress's moral faults with his own. Evidently Shakespeare is in no hurry to treat the final stage of the development, where nothing remains to be uncovered.

In Sonnet 140 the speaker seems ready to exploit his private knowledge of the lady's misconduct by blackmailing her into more kindly behaviour towards him. It is a poem curiously out of key with the conventional distraction of the slighted lover; forceful, direct, and compactly stated. Its opening words of advice to the mistress are as pithy as uncompromising, and have a dramatic bite which Donne might have found congenial:

> Be wise as thou art cruel: do not press
> My tongue-tied patience with too much disdain.

The speaker makes no reference to her looks, and although he briefly assumes the role of dejected lover by mentioning his 'pity-wanting pain', the sonnet's toughness of fibre suggests a controlled contempt for the lady whom it warns, and for whom it contains a veiled threat. In spirit as in sense, 'be wise as thou art cruel', epitomises the scornfully realistic advice offered to the lady by a lover speaking more for her good than his own. If her cruelty presses him too far, he remarks, he may be unable to suppress the wild slanders that will occur to him in his desperation. 'If I might teach thee wit,' he suggests calmly,

THE DARK LADY

better it were,
Though not to love, yet love, to tell me so;
As testy sick men, when their deaths be near,
No news but health from their physicians know.

His advice that she should adopt the wise course of feigning
affection for him is put forward in a disingenuous spirit of
concern. Dishonesty, he knows, will come naturally to her;
and she will readily agree to soothe him with false assurances,
such as are offered a dying man. The simile reminds us that the
lover should himself be close to death; but he is not disposed to
regard this traditional character very seriously. The mistress
must modify her cruelty for reasons of self-interest, not out of
pity for her languishing victim. Made frantic by her disdain, he
might 'speak ill of thee'; and in a world eager to put the worst
construction on idle gossip, she must then expect to fall under
suspicion:

Now this ill-wresting world is grown so bad,
Mad slanderers by mad ears believed be.

This seemingly regretful, even apologetic remark barely covers
a warning that, even if her lover's accusations were baseless,
the lady will be dishonoured by them; and evidently she
realises that his ravings will not be as groundless as he politely
implies. The couplet shows for a moment that his warning has
teeth. 'That I may not be so,' he concludes, meaning that if she
wishes to avoid driving him to this extreme,

nor thou belied,
Bear thine eyes straight, though thy proud heart go wide.

The whole poem represents an astonishingly pointed rebuke to
a mistress whose cruelty has reduced her love to agonised
silence–he is 'tongue-tied' in line 2, however articulate in his
complaint–by her victim, who advises her sardonically to let
self-interest soften her behaviour. Pity will not move her, but

fear of exposure may: let her then wisely abate her cruelty.
Although as lover he remains ostensibly abject, in this address
the speaker assumes a different character; judging the lady's
disdain from a disenchanted standpoint outside the tradition to
which, as lover, he still subscribes. There is nothing tongue-
tied about his ironically deferential offer to teach her the art of
lying to her personal advantage; and nothing respectful of
Petrarchan traditions in his warning that, if she persists in tormenting him, she will bring about not his death but an exasperated disclosure of her true nature. The lover is fighting
back under a bare veneer of courtesy.

His barbed advice, 'Bear thine eyes straight', is explained in
the previous poem, Sonnet 139, to which the speaker is revert-
ing. Here he makes a more conventional appeal for pity, after
imploring the lady not to put him in the position of having to
devise excuses for her unkindness. He produces one, none the
less; explaining that because she knows 'her pretty looks have
been mine enemies',

> from my face she turns my foes,
> That they elsewhere might dart their injuries.

His conceit palliates the fault which the speaker has revealed
plainly enough earlier in the poem. To add insult to the injury
of her disdain, the mistress does not trouble herself to disguise
her interest in other men, even when the wretched lover is in
her company. Like the poet who appeals for a swift *coup de
grâce* in Sonnet 90, the lover begs to be told outright that he is
dismissed, and spared the pain of seeing her openly betray her
new interest. 'Tell me thou lov'st elsewhere,' he asks,

> but in my sight,
> Dear heart, forbear to glance thine eye aside.

He ends the poem by admitting himself already 'near slain',
and by asking the mistress to kill him outright with looks;

seeming to place himself squarely within the tradition which the sequel undermines. But although he has shown his dutiful respect for the lady by inventing a pretty excuse for her unkindness, he has also revealed how shamelessly she is behaving. If he can see her darting looks at other potential victims, he must realise that the lady is not very regardful of her good name; and that the excuse he devises under protest is meant to shield a reputation not worth defending. We do not see the speaker reaching this plain implication; but Sonnet 140 is written as though after an interval during which the point has gone home. The slander which he threatens to utter would disclose the lascivious impulse which he now recognises, in her readiness to attract new admirers before she has cast him off. This explains his warning,

> Bear thine eyes straight, though thy proud heart go wide.

However promiscuous in thought and instinct, she must contrive to look as modest as she is not. The progressive erosion of her moral character has reached the stage where the speaker, although still unable to resist her physical fascination, will soon find nothing to praise in her at all.

In the poems of group (iii) this has happened, and the poet is entirely disenchanted. In Sonnet 130, which catalogues all the respects in which his mistress falls short of fashionable beauty, the speaker is openly contemptuous both of his infatuation and of the defects which he sees with such pitiless clarity:

> I love to hear her speak, yet well I know
> That music hath a far more pleasing sound:
> I grant I never saw a goddess go;
> My mistress, when she walks, treads on the ground.

Beside some of his later tributes, this is mild banter; and the poem is perhaps too deliberate an essay in anti-Petrarchan satire to deserve being so well-known. It comes fully to life in the couplet, where the speaker suddenly rejects indulgent mockery for a more stinging criticism, and reveals his angry resentment:

> And yet, by heaven, I think my love as rare
> As any she belied with false compare.

His indignation is again directed partly at himself, for the perversity of feeling which attaches him to the mistress despite her known worthlessness; increased now by her capacity for lying protestation. In Sonnet 138 the lover accepts her 'false-speaking tongue' without protest, cynically adapting himself to a situation in which each pretends to be deceived by the other, and drawing comfort from a charade which deludes neither of them:

> When my love swears that she is made of truth
> I do believe her, though I know she lies;
> That she might think me some untutored youth,
> Unlearned in the world's false subtleties.

Only a very green beginner could be taken in by so patently false an affirmation; but since it suits his purposes to be considered youthful, he is content to credit her lie – and incidentally, to show his familiarity with the 'false subtleties' in which he vies with his mistress. So, 'vainly thinking that she thinks me young,' although the lady knows that his years 'are past the best', both agree to suppress simple truth in the interest of pleasant relations: the lady's fidelity is not to be challenged, and the lover is not to be reminded that he has outlived his youth. He sums up their mutually tolerant compact:

> Therefore I lie with her, and she with me,
> And in our faults by lies we flattered be.

The equivocation on lying completes the speaker's self-contemptuous explanation. The lady is now indeed his mistress, but in a relationship without passion: he knows her false, and knows that she sees his lack of youth, but neither is disposed to protest at the other's defect. Privately accepting one another as they are, they pretend to be young lovers to whom age and inconstancy are unthought-of, and disguise their awareness of the truth in love-making which acts out the polite fiction agreeable to them both.

The sonnet is an enjoyable *jeu d'esprit;* a witty variation on the main theme of the sequence too shallow in feeling to be closely associated with its neighbours. The disdainful mistress has declined into a complaisant courtesan, prepared to accept a middle-aged lover on her own fickle terms; and the speaker reveals himself as a limp *roué* who would be glad to be thought young, and who adapts himself unprotestingly to the false relationship which both find congenial. The situation has a logical place in the development of the sequence, as it moves away from Petrarchan orthodoxy towards a cynically realistic presentation of love as this tired, insincere liaison of partners too indifferent even to lie convincingly to one another. But Shakespeare treats the situation wrily, and without inviting his reader to become emotionally involved, as he does in the charged writing of Sonnet 129. For the moment, lust remains a subject only for mockery.

A similar jocularity makes itself felt in the equivocal commentary of Sonnets 135 and 136, which are still more damaging to the lady's character. In both the speaker puns insistently upon his name by referring to 'thy Will'; not always alluding to himself. In Elizabethan English, 'will' has the sense of lust;[1] and although the Quarto seems to encourage an innocent reading of both poems by italicising the word and giving it a capital, the speaker's disrespectful purpose is not well hidden:

[1] See *OED will* 2: carnal desire or appetite. See also *Lucrece* 247, *MFM* ii.4.164.

Whoever hath her wish, thou hast thy will,
And Will to boot, and Will in over-plus;
More than enough am I that vex thee still.

[135

He might be saying no more than that the lady has all too much
of her over-persistent and entirely unwelcome lover; but when
he asks later in this sonnet, where the term loses its typo-
graphical disguise,

Wilt thou, whose will is large and spacious,
Not once vouchsafe to hide my will in thine?

only one meaning is possible. The equivocation continues,
though still not leaving his scandalous purpose in doubt, as he
remarks that the sea, 'all water, yet receives rain still'; and
suggests that the mistress should make this her example:

So thou, being rich in Will, add to thy Will
One Will of mine, to make my large Will more.

Word-play confuses the clear sense of the poem to such an
extent that a third character, also named Will, is sometimes
conjured out of the murk; but this carries the speaker's argument further than he intends. Although your lust is already
prodigious, he tells the lady, let me add mine to it and increase
its vastness. His oblique admission of lusting after a thoroughly
dissolute woman develops his cynical description of their
relationship in Sonnet 138, and leads to an eager proposal in the
couplet that the lady shall disdain none of her 'fair beseechers',
but

Think all but one, and me in that one Will.

In the next sonnet he varies his approach; suggesting that if
the lady's conscience troubles her for allowing him 'so near',
she shall

Swear to thy blind soul that I was thy Will.

102

This will be his password, for 'will, thy soul knows, is admitted there.' This welcome visitor, he assures the lady, will fill to overflowing the treasure-house of her love:

> Will will fulfil the treasure of thy love;
> Ay, fill it full with wills, and my will one.

The implication that she is a common resort, with an insatiable appetite for men, is taken up in later sonnets where the speaker's disgust no longer allows him to treat her lust as a matter for indecent punning. Here this approach is light-hearted and irresponsible. He is eager to be accepted as one of the lady's many admirers; and is trying to gain favour by identifying himself with the lustfulness that is her ruling passion. 'Make but my name thy love,' he concludes,

> and love that still,
> And then thou lov'st me for my name is Will.

The speaker too embodies lust, and uses the fact as a recommendation. The breathless appeal of a lover distracted by the freezing remoteness of his mistress is ironically reversed in these two unconventional sonnets, which show their speaker concerned only to persuade a dissolute courtesan to gratify her lust partly through him. Like Sonnet 130, which inverts convention more methodically, they seem to have been written to satirise a current literary attitude; and not in consequence of some private moral lapse. Although it may be difficult to consider Shakespeare, or any other poet, disclosing a liaison so discreditable to his self-esteem, this is not a valid ground of contesting such a reading of these sonnets. The point lies in the poet's ability to make such damaging disclosures under cover of witty badinage. Unlike most of the poems in this sequence –and conspicuously unlike Sonnet 129–they mischievously adopt the point of view of a lover no more disturbed by his mistress's lust than by his own weakness of character; who does not find himself in the agonising position of being fascinated by moral ugliness. This conflict of impulses is barely acknowledged here; and in its absence the poet develops his theme in the direction of comic satire, mocking convention by depicting a flatly unromantic relationship in which suppliant lover and scornful mistress still appear, in a travesty of the exalted ideal which the sequence brings under pressure.

In the sonnets of group (iv) Shakespeare returns to an entirely serious treatment of his theme, and to a mistress whose physical ugliness should–but does not–repel her exasperated lover. Sonnet 141 begins with a characteristically forceful denial that she has any visible attraction:

> In faith, I do not love thee with mine eyes,
> For they in thee a thousand errors note;
> But 'tis my heart that loves what they despise.

His other feelings find her just as unappealing, but neither they nor his reason can dissuade him from loving the woman who plucks the soul out of his body and enslaves him to her will. In the double ignominy of his mad wilfulness and abject servitude he draws comfort only from the pain which the mistress inflicts upon him, as though punishing his perverse behaviour:

> She that makes me sin awards me pain.

There is no need to suppose that 'sin' refers to any other kind of misdeed than the speaker's outraging of reason and inclination, for in this sonnet nothing suggests that he is allowed to make love to his unattractive mistress: to the contrary, the debated line 'Nor tender feeling to base touches prone' seems to mean that she lacks the delicacy that might excite him. Shakespeare has moved away from the situation of group (iii) towards a more conventional form of relationship, where the man can describe himself as the lady's 'proud heart's slave and vassal wretch'; and where devoted service is rewarded not with disdain but with moral self-reproach. There is better reason for seeing the lover involved in a sexual liaison in Sonnet 137, a related poem which continues to develop the painful dichotomy of impulse between his eyes and heart. The angry opening line,

> Thou blind fool Love, what dost thou to mine eyes?

carries the reader directly into the speaker's confusion of feelings, as he finds himself forcibly drawn to a woman whom his judgement repudiates. The 'thousand errors' visible to him in Sonnet 141 are not recognised here, for his eyes now 'see not what they see'; and although familiar with true beauty, mistake the worst for the best. A bewildered questioning of his own irrational behaviour runs through the sonnet to the couplet, as the speaker struggles to understand the perverse desire which he cannot suppress:

> If eyes corrupt by over-partial looks
> Be anchored in the bay where all men ride,
> Why of eyes' falsehood hast thou forged hooks,
> Whereto the judgement of my heart is tied?

This varies the situation of Sonnet 141, where the lover's eyes bring a true report which his heart ignores: his judgement is now at the mercy of senses which are too infatuated to acknowledge what they see, and is led into the same error. Some other part of his mind retains a clear view of the truth, seeing the lady as 'the bay where all men ride': a description which might mean only the cynosure of all eyes, if the verb were not so pointedly equivocal. Its hint is boldly enlarged in the two following lines of Sonnet 135, as the poet renews his shaken self-questioning:

> Why should my heart think that a several plot,
> Which my heart knows the wide world's common place?

Now he refers to the lady's promiscuousness not out of malice but in the course of the self-examination which brings to light the disreputable impulses of his own nature. The poem continues to show him mortified and perplexed by his power-lessness to control the disordered working of his judgement, down to the last angry question why

> mine eyes seeing this, say this is not
> To put fair truth upon so foul a face?

The mistress is no longer the whole focus of the speaker's attention, but a means of disclosing the power of a sheerly impulsive, irrational element of personality to take control of the whole being, in contempt of reasonable judgement. The speaker has good cause for anguished surprise. Contemporary assumptions about the nature and working of man's reason did not allow that the senses might usurp its sovereign authority, or that man's individuality might become hopelessly divided between what he believed or felt and what he knew to be true. Whatever else they may represent, the important sonnets of the Dark Lady sequence show Shakespeare acquiring an imagin-ative understanding of human behaviour which contemporary opinion could not supply. Other factors are involved; not least the concern with dualistic states of being which is so con-spicuous an issue of Shakespeare's early work, in the plays as in the poems. This subject has a place later in this book, where its general relevance to the Sonnets is considered. For the moment it is enough to notice that the conflict between passion and judgement in the speaker of Sonnet 137 is another form of the self-destructive perversity which appears as a theme at the beginning of the whole sequence.

Sonnet 148 is a closely related sequel, expressing much the same tumult of mind and virtually ignoring the mistress as the speaker makes half-frenzied efforts to understand the unco-ordinated behaviour of his mind and senses. Like Sonnet 137, it opens with a bewildered appeal for enlightenment,

> O me! what eyes hath Love put in my head,
> Which have no correspondence with true sight?

and continues to express the speaker's anxiety through a series
of questions which are not answered in the rebuke to 'cunning
Love' which ends the poem. If his eyes do see truly, he asks,
what mad purpose makes his judgement put a slanderous
interpretation on what they see? Evidently 'true sight' declares
the mistress to be ugly, but the speaker's eyes render a different
report: if this impression of her beauty should be true, his
judgement is at fault when it 'censures falsely' what he sees—
or thinks he sees. Continuing to suppose that the lady is truly
good-looking, he asks why this should be commonly denied:

> If that be fair whereon my false eyes dote,
> What means the world to say it is not so?

The private conflict remains; for if the mistress is fair, his eyes
are not false and doting; but the speaker accepts both of these
alternative possibilities. If she is not beautiful, he goes on, his
mistake proves clearly that 'love's eye is not so true as all
men's': the good judgement of common opinion making his
belief absurd in its wrongness. The speaker then springs to
defend himself in a rush of feeling that disorders the metrical
pace of the poem:

> No,
> How can it? O how can love's eye be true,
> That is so vexed with watching and with tears?
> No marvel, then, though I mistake my view.

The glimpse of a sleepless, distracted lover shows a speaker who
is still trying to maintain the attitude and character of his
literary prototype, and who cannot divorce himself from this
tradition of behaviour although he knows himself deceived and
made ridiculous by his credulity. In his doting adoration he is
cozened by his senses, which persuade him to accept as beautiful

a woman generally recognised as ugly and disreputable, and whom his own judgement strenuously resists. The conflict between his mind and senses is deepened by what seems to be an attempt on the poet's part to reconcile a broadly Petrarchan position with the kind of realistic objection to its tenets which the speaker painfully acknowledges. He is in two respects a battle-ground: at war with himself, as sight and judgement dispute the worth of what they together see and know, and struggling to resolve the incompatible attitudes of devoted, cruelly neglected lover and satirically detached analyst which he is made to assume. The couplet gives this tormented sonnet its resolution not by answering the speaker's questions, but by combining these conflicting attitudes in a single statement:

> O cunning Love, with tears thou keep'st me blind,
> Lest eyes well-seeing thy foul faults should find.

The speaker is simultaneously the lover whose tears blind him to the ugliness of his mistress, and the sharp-sighted ironist who knows her 'foul faults'; a realist intent upon discrediting the artificial postures of a literary convention.

His ambivalent attitude is more closely scrutinised in Sonnet 150, where the speaker again addresses the mistress and not his own confused purposes. It is as despised lover that he speaks in the couplet, where he argues that the lady should not scorn him for loving her, as others do, but make his readiness to overlook her faults a reason for treating him considerately:

> If thy unworthiness raised love in me,
> More worthy I to be beloved of thee.

But the lover's plea disguises a pungent satirical comment in which the realist passes judgement upon himself and his mistress together. Since he is dishonouring himself by loving her, he remarks, he is all the more worthy of the favours which would increase his shame. This conflict of impulses dominates the poem, where the speaker asks to be told what gives the mistress her unaccountable power of making evil and ugliness seem attractive:

> Whence hast thou this becoming of things ill,
> That in the very refuse of thy deeds
> There is such strength and warrantise of skill,
> That in my mind thy worst all best exceeds?

His questioning represents an imaginative progression from the main idea of Sonnet 95, where merely to mention the friend's name 'blesses an ill report'; but the moral ambiguity invested in the young man is much simpler and much less confusing to the observer. What gives the friend his popular appeal and masks his moral blemish is evident enough; but the speaker in the Dark Lady sonnets discovers a fascination in the lady which nothing in her appearance or manner explains, and admits himself enslaved by what repels him. In Sonnet 150 he varies his efforts to understand the paradoxical working of his mind by enquiring into the power which enables his mistress to make him

> give the lie to my true sight,
> And swear that brightness doth not grace the day;

a distant allusion to his readiness to regard black as fair. Although continuing to be mesmerised by what he mistakes for her good looks, he knows that he is wilfully denying the truth which his eyes report; for the couplet proves him aware both of her infamous reputation and of the disgrace which he brings upon himself as her lover. But this awareness does not weaken his helpless commitment; rather the opposite, for he asks:

> Who taught thee how to make me love thee more,
> The more I hear and see just cause of hate?

The abject lover of courtly tradition, whose distraction prevented him from making any reliable judgement of his mistress, is joined by a self-contemptuous figure whose infatuated feelings throw his moral discernment out of gear. Although loathing his error, he cannot break free from an attachment which he himself sees as morally humiliating.

Still struggling to break the lady's resistance, he now argues that he deserves the further dishonour of receiving her favours. This equivocal blend of plea and self-reproach appears again in Sonnet 142, which begins by approving the lady's disdain as virtuous, on the ground that it expresses her hatred of the vicious impulse that makes him love her:

> Love is my sin, and thy dear virtue hate;
> Hate of my sin, grounded on sinful loving.

Then, in the face of this moral rebuke to himself, the speaker returns to the role of despairing lover and makes a curious appeal for kindly treatment which requires the mistress to forgo her 'dear virtue' and love the suitor whose admitted perversity should arouse disgust; though not in her. She is a suitable object of his sinful passion, and it should not be she who utters a rebuke of his behaviour. Let her compare his moral condition with her own, the lover suggests, and she will find

> it merits not reproving;
> Or if it do, not from those lips of thine,
> That have profaned their scarlet ornaments,
> And sealed false bonds of love as oft as mine.

The tone of the appeal implies a familiar Petrarchan attitude in the lover, but its substance is remote from any conventional purpose. The speaker concedes that he deserves his mistress's disdain, but through her unworthiness rather than his own: she must substitute kindness for cruelty not out of pity, but because she has no right to comdemn him for faults which she shares: her falseness and inconstancy give him a claim upon her love, since these are his vices as much as hers. The satirical energy of the argument obscures its appeal; but despite the speaker's double attack upon himself and his equally contemptible mistress, he is trying to persuade her to accept the love which he knows—and here proves—to be sinful. By adopting him as lover, the lady will justify the serious imputation which he throws upon her, and deserve the contempt which he already feels for her; but he urges her to overlook the faults in him which she rightly detests, and to accept him on the same lax basis as she adopts in judging her own behaviour:

> Be it lawful I love thee as thou lov'st those
> Whom thine eyes woo as mine importune thee.

This remark picks up the lover's appeal to the lady in Sonnet 139, not to 'glance thine eye aside' in his presence; but he now refers to her coquetry without protest, as a blemish which strengthens his claim upon her. The more vicious he can prove her, the less right will she have to reject him for his 'sinful loving'; but the more he shows himself aware of her corrupt character, the more clearly he reveals his own sinfulness and the perversity of his desire. The argument which should demonstrate that the mistress has no moral right to scorn him proves just the opposite: she has the same cogent reasons for regarding him with loathing as he in respect of her. Like her, he has sworn false oaths of love and lived adulterously, robbing 'others' beds' revenues of their rents'; and to compound these vices he is now ready to equivocate over the moral standards which the mistress has outraged; treating her lasciviousness as evidence of her worthless character, yet proposing to make it justify his own behaviour. Let it be as 'lawful' for him to love her, he proposes, as for her to solicit attention from others while he is struggling to win her approval. His argument is both sarcastic and ironically serious. What the mistress is doing is obviously not lawful; but if her slighted lover may have the same freedom, he will happily regard her behaviour as blameless; though she will then have renounced the 'dear virtue' of her well-deserved contempt for him. He would find this arrangement doubly convenient, for his suggestion admits that he is

pestering her for the same reason as impels her to act provoca-
tively towards other men, and with the same end in mind. The
ironies of 'lawful', both recognised and tacit, cut across the
self-defeating complexities of the argument. To prove that he
deserves her affection and not her hate, the lover exposes the
faults that he shares with the mistress, both condemning himself
and justifying her disdain in the process: her worthlessness and
his deliberate perversity together making nonsense of the convention which inspires his appeal for the lady's pity.

If the poems of the Dark Lady sequence made up a coherent
story, this might be the point at which Sonnet 129 found a
place; as a disgusted commentary by the lover on the subordination of reason and moral judgement by lust. The fact that there
is no such story, and that the poem is an impersonal pro-
nouncement without reference to character, does not mean
that it cannot fit here. Although it evidently suited Shakespeare's
purposes to work out the ideas of the Sonnets within a series of
imprecisely defined narrative situations, he occasionally drops
this device and expresses his ideas directly, as a commentary in
which his two characters are not involved. Sonnet 129 is a case
in point. It stands third in the sequence, unrelated to its context,
and clearly belongs with the poems which have just been dis-
cussed; sharing their concern with the perversity of sexual
impulse, and the helplessness of reason to control its mad
energies. The field of imaginative reference is wider than in
these related sonnets, where Shakespeare seems not to be speaking with his whole voice, or to be working within a more
confined compass of thought. The particular authority of
Sonnet 129 – and, in the main sequence, of Sonnet 94 – seems to
result from a break in the narrative which allows the poet to
discard his role, and to make a much bigger kind of pronounce-
ment over the heads of his characters. In the present instance
the poem proves a massive summing-up of the issue which has
chiefly preoccupied the speaker of the Dark Lady sonnets.

The impersonality of this sonnet means that the poet cannot exploit the conflict of purposes which the lover undergoes in related poems. Instead, the commentary is developed through a succession of strongly marked antitheses, whose effect is very similar to that of the private conflict which makes judgement condemn what 'true sight' acclaims. The whole sonnet is based upon a contrast between the excited impatience of lust and the disgust that follows gratification;

> A bliss in proof, and proved a very woe;
> Before, a joy proposed; behind, a dream.

The same rhetorical figure is impressed upon its commentary. 'Enjoyed no sooner but despised straight' balances opposite ideas in the same fashion as the two lines quoted above, giving them parallel form to emphasise the difference of sense. The same device is used again in 'Past reason hunted ... past reason hated', where the form of the expression is repeated almost exactly, though the two phrases stand in direct antithesis of sense. The second line of the sonnet,

> Is lust in action, and till action lust

does not involve such a contrast of ideas; but by reversing the order of words in the two phrases, 'lust ... action, ... action, lust', Shakespeare makes the line carry a weight of antithesis which deepens the impression of conflict within the poem. The couplet makes use of the same rhetorical figure:

> All this the world well knows; yet none knows well.

The two phrases 'world well knows ... none knows well' balance metrically; there is a direct antithesis between 'the world' and 'none'; and again a reversal of word-order in 'well knows ... knows well' folds the line upon itself, by setting form as well as sense in opposition. The final line rounds off the poem with a further simple antithesis between heaven and hell.

Whatever is true of its form, there is no antithesis of feeling.

The sibilants of the opening line, 'expense of spirit in a waste of shame', renew the revulsion and contempt which the lover feels for himself and his mistress; and the description of lust in a roughly aspirated line,

> Had, having, and in quest to have, extreme;

does not balance ideas but projects them with increasing abhorrence towards a figuratively uttermost 'extreme' that is also an embodiment of the most violent passion. Much the same is true of the mounting indictment which catalogues the qualities of lust, where every additional adjective cuts more spitefully, building up a sense of profound loathing which the poem does not discharge:

> perjured, murd'rous, bloody, full of blame,
> Savage, extreme, rude, cruel, not to trust.

Although such catalogues are a familiar element of Shakespeare's early style, here the inventiveness of the writing is overshadowed by the disturbed verse-movement and the energy of the language, through which the poet voices the disgust which gives the sonnet its driving force. The same feeling shows itself at the end of the octet, where the final word 'mad' is carried over to the next line, to open the sestet. In point of structure, the iterated 'mad, mad', serves to link the two parts of the poem; but what makes the device felt is the savage energy of its comment. If the sonnet is impersonal in respect of having no speaker, it is certainly not detached in feeling. To the contrary, it is a fully committed statement in which the issues of man's sexuality are faced with something akin to masochistic frankness. Its strength of feeling does not mean that Shakespeare had been humiliated by a personal experience like that described in this group of sonnets; though to realise that man does not rule his baser instincts may itself be a humiliation, as it is for Angelo. The other poems of the sequence declare a sustained interest in conflicts which threaten the integrity of the self, by setting up rival authorities of sense and judgement. Sonnet 129 deals directly with the most acute form of this conflict, and ends its bitter analysis of man's subordination to appetite by revealing the fundamental weakness of his moral being:

> All this the world well knows, yet none knows well
> To shun the heaven that leads men to this hell.

His moral awareness has no influence upon his instinctive behaviour, which follows impulse without regard to the protests of judgement, and despite the knowledge that once gratified his desire will seem contemptible. The two basic aspects of his nature are at odds, and cannot be reconciled.

Much the same attitude is central to Sonnet 144, whose ideas are presented in very different form. This is a poem of special interest, as the only sonnet in the whole sequence which refers indisputably to both the Dark Lady and the friend. More than one critic has seen it as a key-poem, though where it should stand in the sequence remains in dispute. From its opening line,

> Two loves I have, of comfort and despair,

and the explanation that follows, it seems that Shakespeare is summing-up the main imaginative concern of the Sonnets: relationship first with the 'man right fair' who is the friend of the first sequence, and then with the mistress 'coloured ill' by whom he is degraded. Such a poem might have been written either to introduce the Dark Lady sequence or to conclude the whole collection; and there is no compelling reason to suppose that one alternative is likelier than the other. It may be significant that here, as nowhere else in the sequence, the poet adopts a position as arbiter; standing apart from the two friends and considering their relationship in detachment from himself. Where other sonnets have treated a triangular relation-ship from which the poet asks not to be excluded, here he expresses no anxiety for himself. Instead, he speculates on the outcome of the lady's attempts to seduce his 'better angel', and resigns himself to live in doubt until the issue settles itself. By presenting the situation in terms of a struggle between the good and bad angels of his own being, in which he himself is not directly involved, the speaker projects his own moral conflict outside himself and becomes its spectator. The nature of the moral conflict described in the sonnets of group (iv) remains unchanged in this new embodiment, which reintro-duces the friend as the personification of the speaker's better self–a development not fully consistent with the character which the first sequence reveals. The inconsistency is suggestive. Over much of the first sequence the friend is a morally am-biguous figure, in whom Shakespeare has prefigured in static terms the moral conflict which becomes actual in the different circumstances of the speaker's association with the Dark Lady. It is the speaker, not the friend, who is then the divided figure attracted and repelled by the same object; and if the friend is admitted to this new situation he can be allowed a character in keeping with his appearance, just as the Dark Lady has been. The situation of Sonnet 144 can then be represented diagram-matically as follows:

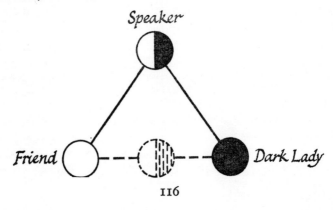

The friend is angelic, the lady diabolical; and the speaker to whom both moral forces belong is a contradictory figure, whose divided nature is self-opposed. Hitherto he has been under constant pressure from both agents, who 'suggest me still'; but a different state of affairs has supervened, in which the good and bad angels become directly related with one another, and ignore him:

> my female evil
> Tempteth my better angel from my side;
> And would corrupt my saint to be a devil,
> Wooing his purity with her foul pride.

This corrupting of the friend's goodness threatens to transform him into a figure as morally divided as the speaker, who being no longer immediately concerned in the conflict, cannot tell whether or not his good angel has succumbed:

> And whether that my angel be turned fiend,
> Suspect I may, yet not directly tell.

His uncertainty creates a phantom-figure of his own divided nature, between the opposite poles of moral being which he suspects may have merged in the friend. The speaker can do nothing to resolve his doubt, but must learn to live in this uneasily divided state of mind until the agents that are both characters in the story and projections of his own moral being themselves resolve their relationship:

> Till my bad angel fire my good one out.

Antithesis is the dominant figure of Sonnet 129, which none the less takes up a sharply committed attitude. In Sonnet 144 the rocking movement of antithesis is felt from the balanced contrasts of the opening lines –

> The better angel is a man right fair,
> The worser spirit a woman coloured ill

–to the opposed equivalents of the couplet; but in this poem there is no declaration of personal bias. The antithetical figures of Sonnet 129 make themselves felt chiefly in the ironic contrast between the impatience of lust and the revulsion that follows: both conditions evoke the speaker's contempt, and give the poem its marked emotional commitment. Of Sonnet 144 one might say that its antitheses are its meaning. The poem consists of a carefully balanced statement describing a state of divided impulse which denies the power of decisive action to the speaker. In its form, the sonnet represents what it describes: the tug of closely balanced but mutually hostile forces within the personality of the speaker, which cannot be settled either way by an act of will, and which he must leave to determine their own outcome. It is in this respect an uncommitted poem. The speaker remains in uncertainty, but is not impatient to learn the truth.[1] We may see the main reason for this acquiescence in his having managed to project a tormenting conflict outside himself. Although the moral struggle is still going on, he has–without entirely ceasing to be its field–receded into the role of spectator, whose double part is now shared between the two strongly contrasted figures with whom he has in turn formed uneasy relationships.

His relationship with the Dark Lady has been characterised by its unwillingness. He is drawn into association with her against his moral judgement, which is revolted by her ugliness and his shameful desire for what he knows to be evil. In this respect his attitude towards the Dark Lady is in direct contrast with his persistent, generally fruitless efforts to establish a close and lasting relationship with the friend. With the young man, whose personal beauty makes the poet eager for intimate friend-ship, he fails to achieve the permanent association he hopes for;

[1] Might it be said that the speaker had discovered himself 'capable of being in uncertainties, mysteries, doubts, without any irritable reaching after fact and reason'?

and sums up his disappointment when he describes himself 'still losing where I saw myself to win.' With the mistress he is generally just as unsuccessful, where winning must involve a greater personal loss. Whether he triumphs in the way Sonnet 151 suggests, or languishes in the mistress's disdain, he is degraded by the relationship, and as anxious to break from her as to bind himself to the young man. A strain of Petrarchan feeling runs through both associations. As suitor to the young man, the poet exposes himself to coolness and inconstancy, and undergoes much the same tortured feelings of grief and hopelessness as the lover in a conventional liaison—a figure which he becomes in the second sequence. His relationship with the Dark Lady either repeats or reverses the form of his previous experience, making it seem an imaginative development of his association with the friend. The circumstances are altered, to produce a story different but closely related: the man is replaced by a woman, beauty becomes ugliness, eager admiration changes to loathing; making one story the reverse counterpart of the other. In this respect the form of the second sequence, and the character of the Dark Lady, are imaginatively implicit in the circumstances of the longer sequence which precedes this complementary story. The Dark Lady takes over, as it were, at the point where the first friendship can no longer provide ground for the interests which Shakespeare has developed. A basis of conventional Petrarchan attitudes persists in the second sequence, and suggests to what extent Shakespeare is still engaged by his original matter. The point of greatest contrast lies in the unwillingness of the lover's association with the mistress. Like the lover's private being, the entity which they might compose, is at war with itself. The first sequence includes some moments of completely integrated relationship, but generally this association too falls short of the achievement the poet seeks. Here again the two sequences are linked by antithesis. The relationship he desires eludes him; the partnership he detests is forced upon him by the perversity of his impulses. Although the form of the experience alters, its essential character remains unchanged; and the drive towards integration fails in the purpose that would unite the opposing halves of a divided being.

CHAPTER FIVE

Truth and Falsehood

E ACH of Shakespeare's works explores a particular field of imaginative attention, its scope indicated by iterative images and terms which reveal where the poet's interests are most sharply concentrated. Like the plays, the Sonnets bring pressure to bear upon concepts peculiar to themselves, which acquire poetic resonance through this treatment. One such concern has its centre in the term 'true', which with related forms of the word makes up a concept mentioned sixty-five times in the Sonnets–far more frequently than in any single play. Through this repetition, which puts the word to use in a variety of different senses, the notion 'truth' is subjected to an intensive scrutiny which searches into its full significance; while the poet carries on a parallel enquiry into the 'truth' of character and behaviour. The interrogation of this key-word of the Sonnets forms an important adjunct to the poet's attempts to unravel the more complex puzzle which confronts him in the friend. This chapter attempts to follow the course of this double enquiry.

It will be helpful to begin by distinguishing five different senses of 'true' which were available to an Elizabethan writer. When the poet promises in Sonnet 123,

> I will be true, despite thy scythe and thee

he indicates the character to which he has conformed during the greater part of his relationship with the friend: steadfast, loyal and constant. These are qualities which he looks for in the friend, but without much success. He has no better luck with the Dark Lady, whose untruth or disloyalty is not disguised. In this

context of ideas, 'true' has a close relevance to the poet's
story; supported by the adjoining sense of honest, sincere and
upright which probably applies in the phrase, 'the marriage of
true minds.' The third meaning of the term is the most familiar
one for modern readers, but evidently holds less interest for
Shakespeare; for it does not appear in passages of any consequence:

> Alas, 'tis true, I have gone here and there.
>   [110

A fourth sense of 'true' signifying exact, correct or right seems
again to offer Shakespeare little imaginative purchase, though
it is employed in the opening lines of Sonnet 148:

> O me, what eyes hath love put in my head,
> Which have no correspondence with true sight?

The most fruitful implications of 'true' evidently lie within a
fifth sense of the word, when it means genuine and not counterfeit; for in all Shakespeare's work the likeness and disparity
that exists between the true and the false constitutes a potent
imaginative theme. The sense in which the friend, the exemplar
of genuine beauty in an age of spurious attractions, yet proves
himself false, is patiently worked out over a considerable
number of sonnets. 'Why should poor beauty indirectly seek
Roses of shadow,' the poet asks in Sonnet 67,

> since his rose is true?

meaning that his beauty is not a product of cosmetics, whose
'false painting' creates only reflected images of the friend's
authentic attributes. This passage, and the related compliment
paid to the friend in Sonnet 68,

> In him those holy antique hours are seen
> Without all ornament, itself and true;

take an important part of their meaning from the context of

ideas built up by the poet's constant sifting of associations. In this way such terms as 'painting', 'shadow' and 'ornament' acquire meanings within the sequence both wider and more particular than they normally possess; and when the poet speaks in Sonnet 24 of finding 'where your true image pictured lies', his remark sets up reverberations in other sonnets which share this imaginative concern with images, true and false. Through them the reader learns to identify the body of interrelated ideas which are implicated in Shakespeare's allusions to truth.

The aspects of truth which concern the poet of the Sonnets most deeply are those of constancy and genuineness. These are the 'true' qualities which the poet claims for himself and proves in his behaviour towards the friend. They are also the attributes which he expects to find in the young man, whose actual falseness the poet gradually comes to acknowledge. Through-out the greater part of the sequence dealing with their friend-ship, the question of the young man's 'truth' in various senses of the word forms a crucial issue of the poet's commentary. At a simple level of evaluation the friend's truth is represented by his beauty: true because, as we have seen, he owes his good looks to nature and not to cosmetics. This is the meaning of the poet's remark in Sonnet 101 that the friend embodies 'truth in beauty dyed'; though it might be right to have some reserva-tions about 'dyed' with its hint of artificiality. The comment has a parallel in Olivia's boastful remark to Viola when the genuineness of her beauty is questioned:

'Tis in grain, sir; 'twill endure wind and weather.

Viola does not contest the claim, but acknowledges 'beauty truly blent', whose colours

Nature's own sweet and cunning hand laid on.
Tw. Night, i.5.258.

Like Olivia, the young man needs no flattering painter's brush to magnify his good looks, for nature has given him an entirely genuine beauty. For this reason the poet can speak of his friend's beauty as though it were synonymous with truth, and credit him with both attributes. He does this in Sonnet 14,

> Thy end is truth's and beauty's doom and date;

and again in Sonnet 101:

> Both truth and beauty on my love depends.

In the second of these sonnets the poet continues by reaffirming the genuineness of his friend's good looks – 'his colour fixed' – and by asserting that a true picture of the friend will not need to exaggerate the qualities that appear so natural in him:

> Truth needs no colour, with his colour fixed,
> Beauty no pencil, beauty's truth to lay.

The truth which 'needs no colour' is not only the beauty which scorns the help of cosmetics: it is the truth of plain fact which can only be expressed in simple language, without the distortions of hyperbole and rhetorical embellishment which the poet condemns in other sonnets. Literary decorum requires the description to be as uncontrived as the beauty which is its subject, for only thus can the poet hope to convey the truth. Exaggerated praise is slighted in characteristic terms in Sonnet 82, which remarks that after the friend's flatterers have exhausted their florid compliments, his own simple praise will be seen to correspond most closely to the truth:

> When they have devised
> What strained touches rhetoric can lend,
> Thou, truly fair, wert truly sympathised
> In true plain words, by thy true-telling friend.

This concern with the truth of poetry transfers attention from the friend's personal attractions to the poet's responsibilities as a writer who must perpetuate a true image of the friend's beauty. One of the problems which confronts him is that of presenting a plausible report. In Sonnet 17 he fears that if he describes the friend justly, readers in some future age will scorn him as a liar:

> And your true rights be termed a poet's rage.

In Sonnet 21, again disclaiming kinship with the type of poet who must seek inspiration in 'a painted beauty', he announces his own standard by pleading,

> O let me, true in love, but truly write.

His own truth is sincerity and constancy of affection, and the truth of his praise a rejecting of the hyperbolic compliment that draws comparisons from 'sun and moon ... and all things rare.' How far Shakespeare himself adopts this critical principle is uncertain. Sonnet 99 is one of several which suggest a quite different inclination. But there is a general tendency for the poet of the Sonnets to censure poetic ornament as well as the forms of cosmetic falseness which he describes in Sonnet 68 as 'these bastard signs of fair.' Set against such spurious images of beauty, the friend's good looks attract praise by their authenticity as much as by their loveliness; which recalls the blossoming of an entirely natural beauty in some previous age which the poet recalls nostalgically:

> Without all ornament, itself and true.

But two sonnets later the same term is used with some ambiguity of sense and purpose. The friend has exposed himself to suspicion and slanderous report; not, it seems, through any fault in his behaviour, but simply by looking so innocently charming. The poet reassures him that slander attaches itself to such persons without guilt:

> The ornament of beauty is suspect;
> A crow that flies in heaven's sweetest air.

But 'ornament of beauty' suggests that the friend's good looks may be only skin-deep, and the term carries implications of spuriousness developed in other sonnets. The image of a crow staining a pure sky strengthens this impression. The friend is a morally equivocal figure, whose beauty must give rise to doubts even while his seeming purity is admitted to be genuine. The poem concludes with a second assurance which leaves the issue unsettled:

> If some suspect of ill masked not thy show,
> Then thou alone kingdoms of hearts shouldst owe.

The ostensible purpose of the poet's remark is to suggest that the suspicion aroused by such beauty acts as a safety-measure, which prevents the friend being swamped by adulation; but his comment can also be read as a rebuke of the vicious trait which a plausible 'show' of outward beauty does not entirely conceal. Were it not for this blemish, the poet tells his friend, you would be the most popular man alive. Shakespeare does not often use 'show' without some suggestion of hypocritical pretence, and here an idea of dissimulation is encouraged by the associations of 'masked' with disguise and self-concealment. The poet is moving, as though unconsciously, towards his discovery of untruth–disloyalty, vicious manners and spuriousness–in the friend who, earlier in the sequence, personifies all the opposite qualities. For Shakespeare himself this development represents a gradual shift of imaginative attention from the immediate aspects of 'truth' in its various simple senses, towards a quickened awareness of the complexities of individual character, whose 'truth' may be impossibly difficult to separate from the false identity which it generates. In this working-out of ideas the friend embodies the qualities of a being whose nature, at first easily defined, proves to be increasingly uncertain and contradictory as the poet explores further. While the speaker attempts to resolve the nature of this elusive reality, Shakespeare brings pressure to bear upon certain key-words of the sequence, as though to test their underlying reality.

In his persistent effort to produce a fitting tribute to the friend's beauty the poet is made to reflect upon two aspects of the spurious. Other patrons do not possess the friend's entirely genuine good looks, but a synthetic charm relying upon cosmetic embellishment: 'the golden tresses of the dead'

> shorn away
> To live a second life on second head.
> [68

When other poets address compliments to the friend or to some other patron, they write flamboyant verse to conceal the insincerity of their purpose, and produce bad art. Sonnet 67 comments on the absurdity of trying to copy the beauty of which he is the only true exemplar:

> Why should false painting imitate his cheek,
> And steal dead seeming[1] of his living hue?

The 'gross painting' which flattering poets apply to their subject, the closing lines of Sonnet 82 assert scornfully,

> might be better used
> Where cheeks need blood; in thee it is abused.

This point is picked up in the opening remark of the next sonnet:

> I never saw that you did painting need,
> And therefore to your fair no painting set.

There are other references to the false art which gives a spurious beauty to the face, whether through cosmetics or poetic flattery, in Sonnets 68 and 127. These allusions to art and painting touch upon Shakespeare's professional interests as a writer, who must maintain a vital concern with forms of imitation

[1] Q 'seeing.' The emendation is well supported.

which despite their insubstantiality cannot be impugned as false. The poet of the Sonnets is made to share this interest when, in Sonnet 84, he offers advice to any writer who wishes to achieve a true poetic style, telling him to match his language to the friend's authentic beauty:

> Let him but copy what in you is writ,
> Not making worse what nature made so clear,
> And such a counterpart shall fame his wit,
> Making his style admired everywhere.

This copying of nature is the basis of art; but what is artistically true is mingled with the underlying falseness of its plausible appearance of reality, as the truth of an actor's performance depends upon his simulating the emotions and temperament of another person. The friend whom the poet believes virtuous and sincere, but later discovers to have only the form of such qualities, epitomises the contradictory nature of art. Thus when the poet tells his friend in Sonnet 96,

> So are those errors that in thee are seen
> To truths translated, and for true things deemed;

he is saying, in the first place, that the friend's dazzling appearance encourages those who notice his faults to regard them as marks of virtuous character; but the notion of mistaking errors 'for true things' shows Shakespeare pursuing a familiar interest in the simulating of reality.

At the beginning of the sequence the poet's entire concern is to persuade the friend to marry and reproduce his beauty. This purpose is soon replaced by a different intention which occupies the poet generally for the greater part of his association with the friend. He is himself to reproduce the friend's beauty through the power of his verse, though his art cannot produce living beings as nature does. The friend might marry any of several young women who

would bear you living flowers,
Much liker than your painted counterfeit.
[16

The portrait and the picture drawn in 'barren rhyme' are lifeless images of the beauty which the young man could propagate
in true images of himself. Through this argument the poet raises
an imaginative theme which works upon Shakespeare throughout his career. The forms and shapes, the 'painted counterfeit'
and the reflected images which reproduce the friend's beauty
in some limited fashion, are kindred figures of the process by
which art attempts to duplicate the substantial world. The forms
assumed by an actor, drawn by a painter or reflected by a
mirror are products of spurious creative activity, set against the
true offspring which the friend could make, were he so minded.
Within this context of ideas, images of the mirror have a
peculiar significance for the young man: they show him the
beauty which he should create anew in a child, and they offer
him an empty reflection which is a worthless substitute for that
substantial form of himself. Sonnet 3 opens with a typical
injunction to

Look in thy glass, and tell the face thou viewest
Now is the time that face should form another.

To refuse to create cheats nature of her due, and involves the
young man in a contradictory relationship with himself. The
idea of his holding a conversation with the reflected image of
his face hints appropriately at narcissism. The face which should
'form another' is a reflection in the young man's mirror; and
although the poet means that he should beget a child of flesh
and blood, he appears to be proposing a mere duplication of
shadows. This notion has its own significance. It is again the
reflection rather than the face itself which interests the poet when
he returns to this theme later in the sequence, and tells the
friend:

Look in your glass, and there appears a face
That overgoes my blunt invention quite;
Dulling my lines, and doing me disgrace.

[103

The friend's beauty is habitually referred to as a shape or appearance rather than as a substantial thing: a painting drawn by
nature's own hand, a true image, a sweet semblance, beauty's
form. Especially in the first fifty or sixty sonnets, allusions to
pictures, paintings, images, shadows and reflected shapes are
frequent enough to make it seem that the friend is an impalpable
and elusive being, more like a figure in a mirror than a solidly
actual person. Several poems encourage this impression by
speaking of him as though he were nothing more than a
picture. 'Mine eye hath played the painter,' the poet begins
Sonnet 24,

and hath stelled
Thy beauty's form in table of my heart:

meaning that by gazing at the friend in adoration the poet has
stamped his picture indelibly upon his heart. The conceit
exemplifies the kind of elaborate compliment which elsewhere
the poet condemns; but in playing with ideas of form, image
and shape the poem suggests that he is not simply involved in a
courtly exercise. The friend is being presented as a private fantasy, given form by the mind's eye; whose beauty is that of a
painting. This still tenuous suggestion of the friend's indistinct-
ness is made again in Sonnet 53, which speaks of him as though
he were a versatile actor whose true self were never disclosed:

What is your substance, whereof are you made
That millions of strange shadows on you tend?
Since everyone hath, everyone, one shade,
And you, but one, can every shadow lend.

This sonnet too might be read simply as lavish compliment:

every legendary figure of beauty finds its true counterpart in
the young man, who personifies all the attractive qualities
claimed for a host of mythological figures. But the question,
'What is your substance?' which might be only an appeal to
the young man to reveal the secret of his charm, includes a
more serious request for him to declare his true identity. Here
Shakespeare's word-game, 'Everyone hath, every one, one
shade', represents the complexity of this personal enigma under
cover of playfulness. The effect of repetition is not to emphasise the singleness of 'one' but to suggest its equivocal
quantity: one is, or may be, more and other than one; which is
how the friend appears to the poet. Although a single being, he
can personate all the millions of 'strange shadows' whose
hearsay beauty he surpasses; yet apparently without appearing
in the solid actuality of his own substance. If he has a private
identity, it seems to be obliterated or lost in the confusion of
shadowy forms into which he projects himself. The extravagant
compliment which provides the surface of the poem overlies
a sense of grappling with illusion which runs through the
sonnet, in its references to shadows, shapes, painting and imitation:

> Describe Adonis, and the counterfeit
> Is poorly imitated after you.

It may not be irrelevant that Shakespeare's Adonis is a sexual
counterfeit: 'no man, though of a man's complexion', and that
the marriage-sonnets describe a miserliness of impulse much akin
to the wilful abstinence of Adonis. Sonnet 53 calls Adonis a
counterfeit ostensibly for a different reason: he is pictured, and
is the spurious claimant to qualities whose genuine form is seen
only in the poet's friend. In the now obsolete sense of 'counterfeit' the poet's comment is unambiguously flattering: Adonis
was modelled on him, but fell woefully short of his example.
In the pejorative sense of 'counterfeit', compliment is replaced

by a wrily discerning appreciation of the friend's personal emptiness: Adonis is a spurious figure–whether sexually or in respect of being a mere picture does not matter[1]–and in this attribute too the friend easily surpasses him. To contest this reading by arguing that Shakespeare obviously intends to praise the young man, and not to dishonour him through equivocal compliments, begs the entire question of Shakespeare's purposes in the Sonnets. The reader must form his own judgement of these purposes, by evaluating the significance of terms which seem crucial to the meaning of individual sonnets. In the present instance, four references to 'shadow' and 'shade' indicate an interest that is amplified by other allusions to insubstantial being, and by the question which begins the sonnet. In Elizabethan usage the term 'counterfeit', conspicuous here, does not always imply spuriousness; but in this context of ideas it helps to sharpen the association of 'imitated' with deceitful appearances. It is hard to resist the imaginative tendency of the poem towards a purpose that has little to do with compliment, though much with Shakespeare's restless concern with form and reality. If we do not insist upon regarding the friend as an actual person, it becomes easier to recognise Shakespeare's working-out of a thematic idea which, in Sonnet 53, is realised through a picture of the poet struggling to grasp the personal identity which the friend conceals behind so many shadowy impostures.

Sonnet 61 shows the poet still trying to resolve a single authentic image of the friend out of a confusing variety of insubstantial likenesses. Unable to sleep, he asks the friend whether he is deliberately keeping him awake:

> Dost thou desire my slumbers should be broken,
> While shadows like to thee do mock my sight?

Initially, the 'shadows' which abuse the sleepless poet are

[1] In the view of Venus, Adonis is both: see *Venus and Adonis* 211–3.

phantasmal images of the friend; but again a second intention presents itself. The bodiless forms 'like to thee' resemble the friend in nature, and not only in appearance; and the mockery which the poet suffers as he discovers the emptiness of the shapes coined by his mind is a disappointment made familiar by the friend's lack of true substance at other times. The idea of the young man's spectral nature is touched on briefly again in Sonnet 27, when the poet tells how his 'imaginary sight'

> Presents thy shadow to my sightless view.

The conceit on blind seeing makes his grasp on this 'shadow' seem still more tenuous. This idea is intensively worked out in the extravagantly witty octet of Sonnet 43, where the poet displays his innate virtuosity in various forms of word-play as he explores the notion of actually meeting the friend whom he sees only in dreams. He sees best with his eyes closed, the poet explains, for during the day nothing seizes his attention; but at night he is united with the friend, and his sight fastens upon this brilliant object in the darkness. He goes on:

> Then thou, whose shadow shadows doth make bright,
> How would thy shadow's form form happy show
> To the clear day, with thy much clearer light,
> When to unseeing eyes thy shade shines so!
> How would, I say, mine eyes be blessed made
> By looking on thee in the living day,
> When in dead night thy fair imperfect shade
> Through heavy sleep on sightless eyes doth stay!

The play on 'shade' and 'shadow' continues, with supporting references to 'form' and 'show', as Shakespeare maintains his pressure upon the theme of plausible likeness. The friend's 'shadow' or visionary figure irradiates the darkness, the poet remarks; but how much more satisfying would be the sight of his 'shadow's form'–the actual being who projects this bodiless shape–in full daylight! Here the compliment is unequivocal; but the idea of failing to come to grips with tangible reality in the friend is still present in the suggestion that the poet has no physical contact with him. In a literal interpretation of the poem, this point would be accountable by the separation which Sonnet 39 appears to admit, and which is more strongly indicated by Sonnet 44. But each of these three poems is open to the kind of figurative reading which imaginative writing invites, and each yields a very different sense to such reading. The intermittent suggestion that the poet cannot establish direct contact with the friend, and that he encounters only shadows, disembodied forms and counterfeit likenesses of the young man, is developed from the questioning of truth and actuality, and their opposites, which runs through much of the sequence. If the Sonnets are rightly taken as a figuring-forth of imaginative ideas, which are given body through the 'story' and its tenuous characters, there is no reason to suppose that any actual separation occurred. The situation was introduced because it allowed Shakespeare to exploit a new aspect of his theme.

From the initial situation of the sequence, where the young man is urged to consolidate himself by marrying–'make thee another self'–the poet admits a series of failures to join the friend to himself in a firm relationship. Physical circumstances or disloyalty repeatedly thwarts his purpose. The friend is absent, or the poet himself goes on a journey; the friendship cools, the poet must be dropped for diplomatic reasons, or a rival usurps his place in the friend's regard. The young man betrays the poet's trust by seducing his mistress, and later the poet wounds the friend by a similar act of unkindness. The poet's appeals for affection, forgiveness or understanding are matched by his constant readiness to overlook the friend's faults, to condone his misdeeds, and even to encourage him to alienate himself. If this record of unrewarded loyalty and patience allows the Sonnets to be regarded as love-poems, they must not be mistaken for an account of love reciprocated. In common with the two narrative poems, they deal with a one-sided attraction and the frustrated wish of a would-be lover to communicate his feelings to an unresponsive partner. In the Sonnets the persistent disappointing of the poet's hopes of achieving a full relationship with his friend helps to promote an impression of the young man's incompletely substantial nature. In a record of actual experience, the idea of a spectral friend would be a conceit suggested by the repeated checks which Shakespeare suffered at the hands of an undiscerning patron. If the Sonnets are to be appreciated as a work of imagination, the idea of a shadowy or equivocal being must be taken seriously. It represents a poetic concept developed from Shakespeare's preoccupation with aspects of 'truth', and invested in a figure of the story through which such concepts are realised.

Hints that the personal identity of the young man is lost behind shadows of himself, or of other personalities which he assumes, are strongest in the sonnets already considered; but the theme makes a tentative appearance very early in the sequence. It is introduced through quibbling allusions to the friend's self which have the effect of implying that he is not in a full sense himself; or that what the poet would regard as the friend's self has become detached from him. Thus Sonnet 13 begins with a heartfelt wish, 'O that you were yourself!' and warns the friend,

> but love, you are
> No longer yours than you yourself here live.

The second line justifies the quibble by reminding the friend that at death he will cease to possess himself; but this does not neutralise the impression that the friend is already incompletely immersed in his personality. Sonnet 4 may explain why the poet should be hinting at this curious possibility:

> For, having traffic with thyself alone,
> Thou of thyself thy sweet self dost deceive.

We should not assume that these repeated references to the friend's individual self involve only a form of verbal conceit. There is of course a play on words; but its purpose is to hammer upon these terms of reference as though to expose their usually unregarded significance. The nature of the friend's private being is in doubt, and the currency of verbal allusion is being struck again and again, to test its soundness within his hearing. The sinister implications of counterfeiting found in later sonnets are not yet heard, but the poet is already speaking of deceit: now used unwittingly by the friend against himself, later to be turned deliberately against the poet. 'You cheat yourself of yourself', the poet remarks in this sonnet; meaning that by refusing to marry, the friend denies himself the perpetuation in a child which–as Sonnet 13 tells him–would assure

> you were
> Yourself again after yourself's decease.

But single life, or more specifically the unnatural practice of 'having traffic with thyself alone,' will deprive the friend of himself in a more ominous sense than a simple reading of the line reveals. The self-love diagnosed by the poet encourages the friend to seek a relationship with himself; and his glass now stands as an emblem of the narcissistic impulse which leads the friend to hoard the beauty which he regards as private property, and to adore his own reflection. Narcissus, Adonis is warned by his loving instructress,

> so himself himself forsook,
> And died to kiss his shadow in the brook.
> [*VA* 161–2

The poet's friend stands in similar danger of confusing the shadow with the substance, and of mistaking the reflected image of his beauty for his real self. The more alarming prospect that underlies the poet's warning is that the friend will deprive his personality of its true self by pursuing the shadow of reflected beauty. Thus in Sonnet 4 Shakespeare is already working on the theme of the friend's indeterminate nature, which becomes a major issue much later in the sequence.

In Sonnet 62 the poet makes a new approach to the topic of self-love by a surprising shift of ground which makes him guilty of the friend's fault. Acknowledging that 'sin of self-love possesseth all mine eye', he admits the kind of complacent opinion that might have been expected of the friend:

> Methinks no face so gracious is as mine,
> No shape so true,[1] no truth of such account;
> And for myself mine own worth do define,
> As I all other in all worths surmount.

But when the poet consults his glass he sees the truth indeed: a face 'beated and chopped with tanned antiquity'; and he berates the self-love which has misled him so absurdly. To justify his mistake, he explains to the friend;

> 'Tis thee, my self, that for myself I praise;
> Painting my age with beauty of thy days.

As in earlier sonnets, the pronoun introduces uncertainties of sense. 'The good looks which I commend as my own,' the poet tells the friend, 'are in fact yours, for you are myself.' His self-love is not sinful, for the attributes which the poet admires in himself belong to his *alter ego*. But the ambiguities resulting from the use of 'myself' to signify 'you' cannot all be resolved by this interpretation. In particular, the remark

> And for myself mine own worth do define,
> As I all other in all worths surmount;

[1] A further sense of 'true' = well-proportioned; cf. *Lear* i.2.8.

leaves the reader uncertain where the poet is referring to his proper self. Evidently he means that when he determines his own worth he assumes the friend's identity, which sets him above all valuation; the phrase 'for myself' meaning that he makes an exchange of selves, as it does in line 13 of this sonnet. The idea of lovers exchanging their selves, or some part of their beings, is not uncommon in Elizabethan poetry;[1] but the complexities of argument developed here are strikingly unusual. Word-play of an advanced kind is characteristic of many sonnets, and the quibbling on 'myself' here might have no further significance; but its effect is to renew the sense of uncertainty about the friend's identity which other poems encourage. The literary conceits of the Sonnets deserve to be thoughtfully considered, for their underlining of imaginative key-words of the sequence. The motif of personal identity which preoccupies Shakespeare in some early sonnets, where the implications of 'yourself' are scrutinised, remains his subject when the focus of attention shifts to a 'myself' which is both the poet and his friend.

The suggestion of a shared personality is presented simply in the couplet of Sonnet 42. To reconcile himself to his mistress's infidelity with the young man, the poet argues that since he and his friend 'are one', the love she gives to the friend proves that 'she loves but me alone.' The baldness of the conceit stands against Dover Wilson's hypothesis that this sonnet was intended to figure much later in the sequence. Its simple working of a current idea relates it to Sonnet 22, which contains another simple form of the same argument:

> My glass shall not persuade me I am old
> So long as youth and thou are of one date.

The second half of the octet brings in the familiar notion of

[1] See, for example, Donne's *A Valediction: of my name*, l. 12: 'Here you see me, and I am you.'

138

exchanging lovers' hearts, using this to justify the poet's claim
to be as young as the friend:

> For all that beauty which doth cover thee
> Is but the seemly raiment of my heart,
> Which in thy breast doth live, as thine in me:
> How can I then be elder than thou art?

Here Shakespeare sets out a basic position from which the more
involved argument of Sonnet 62 is developed: the poet's heart
lives in the friend's body, and so he enjoys its beauty as his own.
Sonnet 39 carries the idea a stage further in a series of rhetorical
questions which show the poet absorbed in the paradox of
shared identity: owning a self which is simultaneously his
own being and another, though always 'myself.' How can he
decently sing the friend's praises, the poet asks,

> When thou art all the better part of me?
> What can mine own praise to mine own self bring,
> And what is't but mine own when I praise thee?

The 'sin of self-love' to which the poet later confesses lies within reach, though the parenthetic gloss of line 4 does not show
the mastery of equivocal statement which other sonnets reveal.
To resolve the impasse, the poet proposes that he and the friend
should live apart; so that the young man should receive his due
of personal praise undiluted by sharing with his second self:

> Let us divided live,
> And our dear love lose name of single one;
> That by this separation I may give
> That due to thee which thou deserv'st alone.

'Not very easy to follow,' Dover Wilson comments of this
sonnet, 'the point at ll.5–8 being obscure.' But the obscurity
is brought about by mistaking the sonnet for an autobiographical statement, and by supposing that 'this separation'

implies an actual parting of the ways between Shakespeare and some noble patron. Obscurity of another kind may be admitted; for the significance of Shakespeare's preoccupation with ideas of true and counterfeit selves, and with the concept of divided being, is obviously difficult to explain. But if the function of criticism is to disclose the imaginative purposes of art, the iterative themes which indicate the poet's persistent interests are a guide to be followed closely, however inconsequential they seem by rational standards. Shakespeare's meaning remains doubtful here, but the sonnet has at least been placed in the context of developing ideas by which it is to be explained. The reader who wishes to understand the Sonnet must look for enlightenment within the sequence, through familiarity with the lines of thought which Shakespeare is seen to pursue.

The half playful proposal of Sonnet 39 that the poet and his friend should live divided–that is, as distinct individuals rather than as a joint personality–follows a suggestion made in Sonnet 36, which has provided a happy hunting-ground for historical speculation. The poet's unhappy recognition

> that we two must be twain,
> Although our undivided loves are one;

varies only slightly from the terms of his proposal three sonnets later; but the argument which follows has been read as an admission that Shakespeare had incurred some official displeasure, and wished to spare his friend the disgrace of associating with him:

> So shall these blots that do with me remain,
> Without thy help by me be borne alone.

Nothing in the sequence supports such a reading. The term 'blots', which has been made to bear such a load of premise, occurs in three other sonnets; in each case as antithesis to an

image of beauty. The allusion to the friend's innocent appearance in Sonnet 95, where 'beauty's veil doth cover every blot',
is a typical contrasted figure of which variant forms are found
in the narrative poems. As the friend is entirely beautiful, so is
the poet completely unprepossessing; and their single being
combines these ill-matching elements in a partnership from
which the poet hopes to draw deep pleasure. But he discovers
obstacles to this satisfaction, even when he has achieved union
with the friend. In Sonnet 39 he recognises that in sharing the
friend's identity, he debars himself from offering the praise
which is the whole subject of his writing; and similarly in
Sonnet 36 he sees what inequality the exchange entails for the
friend. Where the poet acquires the friend's beauty, the friend
gains only the worn and blemished attributes, or blots, which
characterise the poet. The phrase 'my bewailed guilt' in l.10
may imply more than physical shortcomings, but the context
does not encourage us to suppose that the poet has committed a
crime or even behaved badly. More probably the phrase is
merely another form of reference to the personal deficiencies
which make the poet uneasy about sharing a single identity
with the friend. The 'separable spite' which holds them apart is
the complete disparity of nature which, although making the
friend overwhelmingly attractive to the poet, sharpens the
poet's awareness of what poor gifts he can contribute to their
partnership. It hardly needs saying that this argument does not
revolve about any actual relationship. The imaginative centre of
the poem appears to involve a movement of contrary impulses,
which Shakespeare has represented in the conflict of purposes
which seizes the poet as he tries to divide himself from the
friend to whom he is irresistibly drawn. What this may signify
imaginatively will be considered in a later chapter.

Sonnet 37 does not acknowledge difficulties which might
obstruct an integrating relationship with the friend, but takes
pleasure in the thought of the distinguished qualities which the

unremarkable poet gains from the association. Whichever
attributes of the friend seem most desirable—'beauty, birth, or
wealth, or wit'—are acquired by the poet as he sinks himself
in the identity of this other self and loses sense of his own
wretched condition:

> So then I am not lame, poor, nor despised,
> Whilst that this shadow doth such substance give,
> That I in thy abundance am sufficed,
> And by a part of all thy glory live.

The shadow which gives the poet this sense of substantial being
and importance is initially the private fantasy which enables
the poet to project himself into a more richly endowed personality and to forget his personal deficiencies. But in the Sonnets as elsewhere, 'shadow' is often used by Shakespeare as a
deliberately ambiguous term; and here 'this shadow' is not
only the poet's comforting pretence that he is the friend. The
phrase is equally applicable to the curiously insubstantial nature
of the friend, who continually eludes the poet's grasp or proves
out of reach. When the poet assumes this shadowy personality
and acquires its more splendid character and gifts, he follows
the practice of an actor who loses his private self in his role;
but the part he plays is a bodiless concept to which he must lend
his own substance.

The imaginative implications of these sonnets are not likely
to be accepted by those who read the sequence as a personal
diary. To them, the friend is an actual though perhaps unidentified person, and the poet's attempts to make him seem a
wraith are merely sportive. It would be more characteristic of
poetry if the reverse were true. The idea of a half-achieved
relationship with an indefinite, phantom-like being whose
character associates him with dreams, shadows and pictures is
true to the nature of imaginative experience: the notion of an
actual friendship between a poet and a young nobleman is the

material correlative through which Shakespeare indicates the form of his imaginative preoccupation. The meaning of the Sonnets may lie within the significance of ideas which an autobiographical reading discounts or rejects in the mistaken belief that they merely embellish the central facts of Shakespeare's association with William Herbert, or some other distinguished patron. The notion of a shared personality, which such an interpretation must regard as a courtly conceit, persists as a muted theme of the sequence; varying as the poet first shows himself eager to be invested with the friend's beauty and social graces, and then decides to end their relationship to avoid injuring the young man through so unequal a partnership. When he is ready to merge his own individuality with the friend's the poet finds his attempt obstructed by the vagueness of the self with which he is trying to combine. This evasive and almost impalpable quality in the friend is pointed by a continual playing upon ideas of form and shape unaccompanied by any sense of firmly realised actuality. Ambiguity and equivocation, often disguised as compliment, contribute to this impression of indefiniteness. The 'rich praise' of Sonnet 84,

> that you alone are you,

is typical of the poet's habit of eulogising the friend in terms which admit of very different interpretations, and which offer no reliable guide to the friend's true nature. This equivocal comment is repeated later in the sonnet, when the poet remarks as though stating a simple truth:

> But he that writes of you, if he can tell
> That you are you, so dignifies his story.

The intention may be as simple as it seems: the friend is the nonpareil of beauty, and to give his verse distinction the poet need only describe him as he is. But even when the task is stated in these plainer terms its difficulty is admitted; for what is the friend? Readers who have recognised the range of Shakespeare's imaginative interest in the theme of identity, which leads him to examine acting, simulation and hypcritical seeming as concepts related by their common bearing upon truth and falsehood, will not easily put this implicit question aside. The poet tries to identify the friend, and fails; baffled by the multitude of 'strange shadows' which seem to constitute his being. These are not fanciful terms which must be scaled down before they become intelligible as references to the noble patron whose tantalising remoteness Shakespeare admires and regrets, but an immediate indication of the imaginative subject which he is treating. As the poet tries to establish the true nature of his shadowy partner, Shakespeare gives poetic form to his awareness of contradictions within the individual self which make it impossible to separate truth from its spurious counterparts. A reader who wishes to follow either endeavour with understanding must resist the inclination to re-state their imaginative interests in more readily comprehensible terms. The Sonnets are not easy. Whether they offer us direct contact with Shakespeare's private thoughts or not, we should be prepared to read them with the watchfulness that great writing demands, and with respect for the integrity of their poetic expression.

CHAPTER SIX

Increase and Creation

BOTH in the Sonnets and in the two narrative poems the idea of creative activity has a central importance. Tarquin has no desire to beget a child upon Lucrece, but the energies he liberates in his lustful attack are those of procreation, bestially transformed by their divorce from moral restraint. Venus is eager to initiate Adonis into sexual maturity; not apparently for the pleasure of herself bearing his child, but so that he will put his creative power to use by reproducing the beauty lent to him. In her attempt to convince him she relies less upon her personal fascination than upon the force of moral argument, proving his obligation to spend himself sexually to repay Nature's generous endowment:

'Upon the earth's increase why shouldst thou feed,
Unless the earth with thy increase be fed?
By law of nature thou art bound to breed,
That thine may live when thou thyself art dead.'
[169–172

Her moral rebuke anticipates the form of the poet's remonstration against the friend's abstinence, and employs some of the same arguments. The friend is as obdurate as Adonis; and although the poet seems initially to share Venus' persistence, he eventually gives up his efforts to prise the friend out of his self-imposed abstinence, and the theme of creation seems to drop out of the sequence. But although nothing further is heard about marriage and children in whom the parent's youth is renewed, the theme is not discarded. After the original ideas have been thoroughly scrutinised in the opening group

145

of sonnets, where there is less shift of position than in any other section of the sequence, Shakespeare develops the theme very rapidly; pursuing the implications of the young man's behaviour to a point where his individual nature has been fully analysed. In respect of imaginative development, this gradual disclosure of hypocrisy in the friend cannot be taken to represent the analysis of an actual personality. The ideas thus linked together seem to derive from Shakespeare's imaginative experience, and to form a pattern private to his work which is impressed not only upon Adonis and the friend of the Sonnets, but upon several dramatic figures. In discussing any one of these wilfully abstinent characters we are in effect discussing them all, for differences of sex and social status have little bearing upon the pattern of behaviour to which they all conform. The friend of the Sonnets is perhaps the most closely studied of these figures, and with Adonis the imaginative prototype of a being who reappears in characters as outwardly unlike as Angelo and Olivia. In all of them self-love is at least potentially a force of self-destruction, through its perverting of the creative power that is the source of man's greatest energy.

Shakespeare's interest in this thwarting of creative impulse could be taken as evidence of a direct concern with man's psychological behaviour; but although it would be foolish to question Shakespeare's deep intuitive understanding of human nature, it is probably mistaken to suppose that the promptings which shape his characters originate in this understanding. What he creates comes from his imagination, and conforms with conditions brought into existence by the same creative impulse; as the world of Cyprus exists as imaginative complement to the figure of Othello, not as a neutral background to his actions. The psychology of his narcissistic characters may be true to type, but this matters less than its truth to Shakespeare's imaginative purpose; for we do not read his work to be informed about the nature of everyday life or to be instructed in clinical psychology, but to undergo the imaginative experience which his poetry transcribes. If he seems to propose moral attitudes, as he does when he makes Venus censure Adonis's refusal to spend his creative potential, Shakespeare is not offering guidance to his readers but defining the conditions by which Adonis is to be judged. When Viola rebukes Olivia for the same fault we recognise familiar surroundings: a corner of private territory to which Shakespeare returns for a moment, to run over ideas that form a constant feature of his imaginative outlook:

> *Viola:* Are you the lady of the house?
> *Olivia:* If I do not usurp myself, I am.
> *Viola:* Most certain if you are she, you do usurp yourself;
> for what is yours to bestow is not yours to reserve.
>
> [*TN* i.5.198–201

The warning that Olivia does usurp herself is as cryptic as the remark that follows: a compact summary of the moral argument advanced against the friend who threatens his own existence by refusing to marry. Like him, Olivia has adopted a miser's attitude towards the personal beauty which she regards as her own property, to be withheld from use as she wishes. Shakespeare barely allows his audience time to take the point, which although fully elaborated elsewhere is too compressed here to explain itself in performance. The Duke of *Measure for Measure* sets out his version of the moral argument in a more leisurely manner; but although less cryptic his speech conceals its warning almost completely under a bland impersonality of comment:

> Thyself and thy belongings
> Are not thine own so proper, as to waste
> Thyself upon thy virtues, they on thee.
> Heaven doth with us as we with torches do;
> Not light them for themselves.
>
> [*MFM* i.1.29–33

147

The relevance of his remarks cannot appear until Angelo is revealed as another figure whose pride restrains the impulse of self-spending and denies expression to his creative energy. He falls victim to lust much as the related figure of Adonis is savaged by the boar; and in offering to release Isabella's brother in return for her chastity Angelo proves himself a double hypocrite. Olivia is exposed to a different kind of humiliation. Her becoming infatuated with the disguised Viola involves no moral disgrace, but makes her ridiculous in her failure to distinguish between the shadow and the substance of Viola's identity. The pride that impels a sterile relationship with a mirror-self leads to an inability to form meaningful associations within the world of substantial being. In the darkness of Mariana's summer-house Angelo encounters a woman who is the shadow of Isabella, and wastes his sexual potential upon an impostor whom his own self-ignorance has helped to create.

These dramatic figures embody later and more complex developments of a theme which in the Sonnets Shakespeare is only beginning to elaborate; but it can be helpful to look ahead to the fully realised expression of his early ideas. Two examples do not adequately suggest the extent to which the plays are permeated by imaginative concepts reached by an intensive working-out of the simple ideas that provide Shakespeare's starting-point; but to follow their development in any detail would require a separate study. Here it is possible only to suggest that the theme of self-ignorance which forms a massive issue of *King Lear*, and the wider concern with identity which is almost never silent in the plays, stem from interests in Shakespeare's early poetry which become increasingly vigorous as they are explored; and that in *King Lear* the thwarting of creative potential which Shakespeare associates with self-love is a theme which triggers writing of an almost terrifying imaginative power. Not merely the persistence of these early ideas but the dynamic energy which they acquire show what a vital poetic impulse was finding expression in the opening group of sonnets, as the poet warns and argues against the friend's perverse determination to remain unmarried.

The cause of this perverse impulse is revealed in the first sonnet, immediately after the statement of the moral positive which the friend has elected to ignore: the desire for increase. Instead of choosing a feminine partner who will return the affection he lavishes on her, the friend enters into a loving relationship with his own image; spending fruitlessly the energy which marriage would put to creative purposes:

> But thou, contracted to thine own bright eyes,
> Feed'st thy light's flame with self-substantial fuel;
> Making a famine where abundance lies.
>
> [1

As a victim of self-love, the young man is committed to delusion: initially in mistaking the mirror-self for a true being, and spending himself upon this shadow; and secondly in supposing that the beauty which he admires is his own. In Sonnet 4 the poet tries to correct this mistaken belief by reminding the friend that nature 'gives nothing, but doth lend', and that her generous gift requires him to be equally open-handed. He also warns the friend that self-love will not only deny him the pleasures of natural increase but commit him more deeply to delusion by calling the reality of his true being into question:

> For, having traffic with thyself alone,
> Thou of thyself thy sweet self dost deceive.
>
> [4

He cheats himself of the living child in whom he would see himself truly reproduced; and the friend also deprives himself of substance by transferring his identity to the mirror-self for whom he feels such regard. Some few poems later the note of warning sharpens, as though the poet now feels that the friend

149

is bent not simply upon leading himself into delusion but upon destroying himself. Protesting at the friend's evident intention of inflicting 'such murd'rous shame' upon himself, the poet argues that a man with such suicidal purposes cannot be expected to bear love towards others. The next sonnet repeats and extends his argument, adding a new feature to the character which the poet is gradually disclosing:

> For shame deny that thou bear'st love to any,
> Who for thyself art so unprovident;
> Grant, if thou wilt, thou art beloved of many,
> But that thou none lov'st is most evident.
>
> [10

While in point of story the poet's criticism is merely playful–if he believed the friend to be incapable of affection there would be no reason to prolong their relationship–the suggestion that the friend loves no one is imaginatively important. At a common-sense level the poet's comment is justified by the selfishness of the friend's impulse to give nothing of himself away, and to hoard up his natural gifts for his own private use. The poet's argument shows that this self-love is not in fact self-regarding; and suggests that the friend is not preserving but wasting himself by his infatuated attachment to his own good looks, whose reflected image is in a double sense nobody. Whatever capacity for loving the friend possesses he spends upon this nobody, who absorbs his whole attention; and in this absorption he loses the power of projecting himself creatively through relationship with others. Although 'beloved of many' for his immediately attractive appearance, by his infatuation with a shadow the friend is denying himself the ability to return the creative force of love; so that while his appearance suggests the vital potentiality of a lover, the course which the friend has chosen will transform him into a figure as sterile and unproductive as the relationship he has induced with his

mirror-self. In this respect he and Adonis will the same consequence of self-love upon themselves, and deserve the same
scornful rebuke:

> 'Fie, lifeless picture, cold and senseless stone,
> Well-painted idol, image dull and dead,
> Statue contenting but the eye alone,
> Thing like a man, but of no woman bred!'
>   [*VA* 211–14

What begins as a disinclination to spend the creative potential
of the self leads to a delusive association with a shadow-self,
and ends in sterility.

A further point now emerges from the poet's mock-serious
scolding of his friend. Although he seems ready for marriage
and parenthood, the attractive figure which he presents is a
sham, effectively neutered by his miserly hoarding of the sexual
energy which he should give away. The friend is thus an
equivocal if not hypocritical being, whose outward appearance
gives a seriously misleading account of his inward nature.
From this early point in the sequence Shakespeare begins to
hint at the duplicity in the young man which later sonnets
bring to light: a quality which seems to be imaginatively
implicit in the friend's refusal to marry which forms the
starting-point of the long investigation of his nature. His
duplicity is most obvious in his betrayal of the poet later in the
sequence, but this merely confirms a feature of his character
silently indicated in the early sonnets. The friend deceives
himself by wasting his reproductive energy upon a shadow;
he cheats nature of her proper return by refusing to pay back
her loan in a child, and by dividing himself between the
substance and the shadow of his being he acquires a doubleness
of person–himself both lover and beloved, actor and admiring
audience–that is complementary to his hypocritical behaviour.
It may be difficult to associate these metaphysical ideas with a

conception of human character, but we have to resist any inclination to regard Shakespeare's thought-process as a display of ingenuity designed to flatter and amuse some actual friend. The young man has no more existence than the Sonnets give him in the course of resolving the ideas which Shakespeare's imaginative searching brings together. They, and not the young man, are the vital matter of the sequence: the product of a restlessly creative mind recording its own movements of attention, and using the young man as a lay-figure who can be made to accommodate its associations of idea. He exists in terms of these imaginative associations alone, not as some actual person upon whom Shakespeare has piled fantastic compliment which might be stripped away to reveal a true being.

Sonnet 20 varies the terms in which the friend is presented, but continues to insist upon his doubleness. As 'master-mistress' of the poet's emotions he is at once both male and female; and able to evoke in the poet both the affection of a friend and the passion of a lover. A man 'in hue' or shape, he has a feminine beauty which men find strongly attractive, while women are equally drawn by the appeal of his masculine attributes. To explain this hybrid nature the poet tells how the friend was first intended for a woman,

> Till nature as she wrought thee fell a-doting

and absent-mindedly added the genitalia of a man. So far as the friend retains certain feminine characteristics, he possesses only their attractive aspects without the usual shortcomings of women:

> A woman's gentle heart, but not acquainted
> With shifting change, as is false woman's fashion;
> An eye more bright than theirs, less false in rolling.

Only an oddly imperceptive reader could mistake this sonnet

for a complimentary address. Few men, however good-looking, would enjoy being told that they were designed to be women; and one who had just reached manhood would be still less amused if his sex were called into question, however wittily. If we put aside the unlikely suggestion that the poem is addressed to Shakespeare's patron, and allow its ideas the importance they deserve, we may recognise what damaging criticism the sonnet contains. Like Adonis, whom Venus describes as 'more lovely than a man', the friend enjoys his unusual beauty at the expense of the sexual drive that characterises manhood–not surprisingly if, as the poet asserts, his genitalia were added as an afterthought. Neither man nor woman in an effective sense, this blended being is sexually neutral; and although immediately attractive in both his male and his female aspects, he is incapable of fulfilling either sexual role. Like the Angelo of Lucio's disrespectful report, he is 'a motion generative'; having the appearance and seeming capabilities of a man, but in fact a plausible puppet able to make only the gestures of creative potency.

Here as earlier in the sequence, the poet associates the friend's equivocal sexual nature with hypocrisy and double-dealing. In Sonnet 20 he reassures himself that although the friend has the delicate beauty of a woman, he is without the fickleness and inconstancy that characterise feminine behaviour. In this attempt to secure himself the poet ignores the warning signs of divided being which he himself noticed previously. Even without the bisexuality which is so clear an index of the friend's contradictory nature, a man who has

all hues in his controlling

must be able not only to attract men of every kind, but to adopt any shape at will. It would be easier to resist the implications of this ambiguous phrase if later episodes of the sequence did not reveal the friend's duplicity; or if Shakespeare's idea of the young man did not associate self-love with deception from the first sonnet. If we suppose that Shakespeare was telling his own story in the Sonnets, and that he did not recognise the friend's hypocrisy before their relationship reached the stage represented by Sonnets 93–95, we make him incapable of realising the full significance of his initial comments on the friend's refusal to marry. It should be obvious that when he associates self-love and stubborn abstinence with sexual counterfeiting, and identifies the friend as a bisexual being whose nature is in conflict with his appearance, Shakespeare is not analysing the character of an actual person but exploring a complex of ideas which his creative consciousness holds together. In real life there may be no reason why a young man who becomes enamoured of his reflection should be incapable of reproducing himself sexually, but Shakespeare is not writing a study of narcissism and its consequences. His imagination seizes upon a metaphorical relationship between the mirror's propagating of false forms – true in appearance but bodiless – and the making of genuine offspring through marriage, where the child reflects the father's appearance in living substance; and this association of ideas provides the basis of an imaginative appreciation which he develops much further. As a poet, Shakespeare has persuasive reasons to pursue this connection of ideas as far as it can be followed; for both the true and the false forms of propagation which he contrasts are associated by analogy with his own creating of human figures in drama: beings who are both living progeny and shadows.

Here it can be illuminating to remind ourselves that, whether he speaks for Shakespeare or not, the poet of the Sonnets follows the same calling and shares his professional interests. He too is a maker; and when the poet encourages his friend to reproduce himself, he asks him to commit himself to a form of creative activity analogous to his own poetic making. This parallel is enforced through images which allude to natural increase and procreation in terms of conscious art and craftsmanship. Sonnet 11 tells the friend that nature

> carved thee for her seal, and meant thereby
> Thou should'st print more, not let that copy die.

Five sonnets later the poet concludes a comparison between the means by which either of them might perpetuate the friend's beauty by advising him,

> you must live drawn by your own sweet skill.
> [16

The poet will do his best to eternise that beauty through the living memorial of his poetry; but he reminds the friend that he has himself a power 'more blessed than my barren rhyme', which will keep his beauty alive and youthful in a form more substantial than art can fashion:

> So should the lines of life that life repair,
> Which this time's pencil or my pupil pen
> Neither in inward worth nor outward fair
> Can make you live yourself in eyes of men.

In Sonnet 17 the couplet repeats the association of sexual increase with poetic making, drawing an almost explicit parallel between the two kinds of activity:

> But were some child of yours alive that time,
> You should live twice; in it and in my rhyme.

The poet has other reasons than those of personal affection for wishing to keep the young man's beauty in being. He sees his professional task as an endless struggle against 'this bloody tyrant, Time', whose destructive purpose can only be frustrated by the creation of fresh beauty or by the process of art which holds life suspended. This process is symbolised through images of distillation which provide an equally potent means of representing the perpetuation of personal essence through a

child. The metaphor is introduced in this sense in Sonnet 5;
where after warning the friend of the wintry bareness which
must follow the green summer of his youth, he continues:

> Then were not summer's distillation left,
> A liquid prisoner pent in walls of glass,
> Beauty's effect with beauty were bereft:
> Nor it, nor no remembrance what it was.

The further significance of 'summer's distillation', the lasting
perfume extracted from the flowers by process of art, is not
yet admitted: for the moment Shakespeare is taken up with
the idea of an individual essence that is kept alive through
procreation. In the next sonnet the poet develops his argument
by telling the friend not to grow old before his youthful beauty
has been distilled:

> Make sweet some vial, treasure thou some place
> With beauty's treasure ere it be self-killed.
>
>   [6

From this delicate allusion to the child's mother it appears that
Shakespeare is widening the scope of his image so that the
distillate represents both the child and the sexual essence of the
friend; but without hinting at the separate analogy with his
own distillation of beauty. This finds a place a good deal later
in the sequence, though in a context of ideas directly related
to the argument of these early sonnets. It is now the poet who
appears in the role of distiller; promising that as 'sweetest
odours' are extracted from roses when they wither, so he will
preserve the friend's youthful beauty:

> When that shall fade, my verse distills your truth.
>
>   [54

The metaphor which previously stood for procreation is now
applied to poetic making; and we recognise that where it is
first employed in Sonnet 5, 'summer's distillation' can be

understood in both senses; either as a child or as a poem praising–and perpetuating–the friend's beauty. By this open imaginative link between writing a poem and begetting a child, Shakespeare encourages us to see one activity in terms of the other. The creative energy of the poet will give being to an undying image of the friend; and in much the same way the friend will defeat time by reproducing himself as a living figure of his own youth. This, at least, is the positive which the poet recommends to his wilfully abstinent friend.

The argument is enlivened by its levity, but Shakespeare is treating ideas of close concern to himself as poet. The process of artistic creation is a subject whose fascination is greatest for those who undergo the experience of making, in whichever medium. The poet cannot be a maker without being aware of the unusual power which separates him from other men, and from his own everyday self; though the source and nature of this creative ability may lie beyond his comprehension. Such evidence as poetry and painting provide suggests that those who possess outstanding creative power are irresistibly drawn to this subject, and impelled to represent the nature of their creative experience as a means of understanding it. For this reason the poet's search for forms of activity analogous or parallel to his own making may provide a motive of his greatest–because most imaginative–writing. To the critic, the nature of such experience must remain obscure, to be grasped inductively and at second hand by studying its imprint upon the work which it impels. The more profound the experience, the clearer these indications are likely to be; and in the work of Shakespeare we might properly expect to notice a sharply conditioned response to topics which bring him imaginatively close to his own activity of making. Of the possible analogues, that of pro-creation represents this process in the most immediate and powerfully charged metaphor of the creative process, repre-senting–the layman may suppose–not only the peculiarly vital nature of the happening, but the deep excitement which accompanies it. In point of imaginative association it seems inevitable that as the poet of the Sonnets sets himself to preserve 'beauty's rose' from time, he should encourage the friend to use his sexual potential in the same task. In begetting a child, the friend will second the poet's creative activity. Both are to be makers.

But the young man refuses to become a partner in this undertaking; and instead of creating living progeny through marriage, he shuns feminine company and initiates an admiring relationship with himself. Where he should reproduce himself in flesh and blood, he creates only a duplicate figure of himself in his mirror. Shakespeare's interest in this mockery of true creative activity is no less marked than his imaginative awareness of alternative forms of making. In knowing himself to be a maker who possesses an entirely genuine power of imparting life to his creatures, he seems also to be conscious of a complementary being who is perhaps an aspect of himself, who claims the same kind of creative ability but whose making is altogether fraudulent. Shakespeare's consciousness of this impotent but plausible being, whose characteristics are embodied in several of his dramatic figures, may be sharpened by his admission that the men and women he sets upon the stage are in themselves no more substantial than images in a mirror; for as Theseus remarks,

> The best in this kind are but shadows.

Yet Theseus is himself such a shadow; and the paradox of Shakespeare's art is that it endows such bodiless figures with such vitality that they outlive the poet and their time. In this regard the friend of the Sonnets, who makes only lifeless shadows of himself, displays the characteristics of a bad poet whose figures gabble and gesticulate as though soundlessly. In a true poet, an awareness of this counterfeit making seems to be a related part of his recognition that he possesses creative power. The idea of the facile process which merely simulates the vital making of poetry or of procreation is never far from Shakespeare's mind when he contemplates these allied forms of activity. In a scene of *Measure for Measure* which contains some striking references to procreation, Isabella speaks depreciatingly of women's frailty; seeing a parallel with 'the glasses where they view themselves',

> Which are as easy broke as they make forms.
>
> *MFM* ii. 4. 129

In this effortless making of forms women and mirrors may be equally adept, but they do not both entail genuine creation. When the young man refuses to spend his sexual energy upon natural increase and binds himself instead to a mirror-self, he not only rejects the poet's offer of creative partnership, but substitutes for it a trivial and delusive form of the same activity. The poet's anxiety that his friend should marry is the outward expression of an imaginative concern with true and false modes of making, which engages Shakespeare's attention deeply.

This interest probably helps to explain why Shakespeare made the speaker of the Sonnets a poet, and why the friend is his negative counterpart: self-loving, sexually ambivalent, and creative only to the extent of duplicating lifeless images of himself. The two characters are antithetical in so many respects that they can be regarded as opposite aspects of the same being; nowhere more than in the marked contrast between the genuine creative ability of the poet and the impotence of the friend, who squanders himself in self-admiration and refuses to beget substantial offspring. For those who believe that Shakespeare's capricious patron was in truth unlike the poet in every respect, it may be helpful to recall that Viola and her brother Sebastian are involved in a dualistic relationship of just this kind. When

brother and sister are eventually set side by side, Viola still
dressed as a man, the Duke finds it impossible to distinguish
between them:

> One face, one voice, one habit, and two persons;
> A natural perspective, that is and is not.
>
> *TN* v.i. 223–4

As the mock-man Cesario, Viola impersonates her brother
capably enough until she is required to give proof of her
masculine spirit; but her complete lack of mettle, both as a
duellist and as a lover challenged by Olivia's proposal of
marriage, reveal the sexual imposture which she has attempted.
With Sebastian's arrival this spurious figure of manhood is
displaced by its genuine counterpart, who proves his credentials
where Viola has failed; humiliating his assailants and immediately taking Olivia as his wife. Outwardly the twins seem
to be the same man; but one is as counterfeit as the other is
authentically male, and the charming masculine guise adopted
by Viola collapses under pressure, to reveal an equivocal being
who lacks the characteristic vigour and drive of a man. Between
Sebastian and Cesario, whom the Duke is ready to acknowledge
as alternative forms of the same person, there exists a relationship closely similar to the curious association which links
together the poet of the Sonnets and his friend. Cesario seems
capable of sword-play and of marriage, but is a sexual hybrid
incapable of either activity; while his *alter ego* Sebastian
demonstrates his masculine prowess in both. In his sexual
vitality Sebastian is the positive counterpart of his indeterminate double; just as the poet of the Sonnets reverses the
negative qualities of his uncreative friend, whose manhood is
mere semblance. The imaginative figure persists, as Shakespeare continues to explore an essentially poetic concept drawn
from his awareness of the creative self.

The Sonnet's linked figures of true and counterfeit creative power hold an obvious significance for a poet whose great career has recently begun. Shakespeare is already conscious of the abundant creative gift that will keep his work alive to future ages; and so possessed by his experience as maker that he may find it hard to exclude this awareness from his poetry. His interest is clearly, if obliquely, acknowledged within the story of the first twenty sonnets, where the speaker asserts the moral positive of natural increase and self-spending which the friend denies, preferring to waste himself despite the poet's warnings. His moral authority gives the poet the more conspicuous place in the story and makes it easier to suppose that he speaks for Shakespeare; but imaginatively the friend is the more important figure. Through him Shakespeare deepens his enquiry into the nature of creative consciousness, by allowing the poet to discover in the friend the guises adopted by the spurious agency which offers itself in place of creative power, and whose progeny has no life of its own. Perhaps Shakespeare is suggesting that the true poet is coupled with another being like himself in all respects except this vital one, who simulates his activity as maker in a mock engendering; spending his energy upon himself to people his private world with shadows. Other poets who have tried to look into their creative consciousness and to discern its workings have found a similar figure of counterfeit vitality coexisting with the representative of generative power, from which it seems inseparable. The critic can do little more than gesture towards the implicit significance of these linked figures in the Sonnets, whose meaning can only be grasped through an understanding of the imaginative experience which has produced them both.

After Sonnet 20 there is no further allusion to the friend's lack of sexual drive; and hints later in the sequence that he has seduced the poet's mistress and earned a reputation for lasciviousness suggest that his nature has changed radically. Not his character, but Shakespeare's purpose has altered. The theme of sexual abstinence and self-love has been worked to the point where other motifs come into view, and Shakespeare has transferred his interest to the idea of duplicity developed from these opening sonnets. It is now that the poet finds it difficult to come to grips with the friend's substantial being, finding him manifested as a picture, a phantom, or a reflection in a glass, and never as a solidly actual presence. He is set 'in limits far remote' from the poet, who searches for his image 'in some antique book' and asks whether the friend's spirit could be sent 'so far from home' to watch his movements. By being too self-infatuated to marry, and content to duplicate his beauty in a mirror, the friend has become as tenuous and impotent as the shadow-self which he admires. Although Shakespeare's attention has moved away from the marriage-theme and its immediately related ideas, his imagination is continuing to develop lines of interest drawn from the poetic basis of the sequence. He does not explicitly associate the disembodied condition of the young man with the narcissistic love which the poet diagnoses earlier: this feature of the friend too has receded, and although self-love remains a motif of the Sonnets, it is now expressed in the poet's devoted affection for the second being whom he regards as himself. None the less, the shadowy vagueness of the friend is an idea plainly developed from the first group of sonnets; and the curious relationship which comes about between the sharers of a single self is similarly an extension of the early paradox about the young man's attachment to himself. In this way the later sonnets build up their uneven story by working out the poetic implications of concepts introduced by the opening argument of the sequence.

The idea of the friend's loving relationship with himself suggests that he has a double nature; and this doubleness contains the notion of duplicity. He already cheats himself by wasting his substance upon a shadow; himself becoming a shadow whose want of solidity and definiteness is symbolic of

INCREASE AND CREATION

the equivocations of his personal behaviour. In Sonnet 92 the poet nerves himself to acknowledge the friend's disloyalty which he has been struggling to conceal from himself:

> But what's so blessed fair that fears no blot?
> Thou mayst be false, and yet I know it not.

In the next sonnet the poet seems to have abandoned pretence, and envisages himself as the unsuspecting victim of his friend's deceit,

> supposing thou art true,
> Like a deceived husband.
> [93

He now treats the friend's dissimulation simply as an index of his moral character, without suggesting that his doubleness takes any other form. The friend's beauty, the poet now realises, masks him; and his expression is unrelated to the shifting emotions within. The poet seems to be paying the friend a compliment when he tells him that

> heaven in thy creation did decree
> That in thy face sweet love should ever dwell,
> Whate'er thy thoughts or thy heart's workings be.

But it cannot be praise to imply that he is a born hypocrite, and that his face is immoveably fixed in a semblance of affection that he does not feel. Although Shakespeare's initial conception of the friend as a sexless being is now some way behind, in this sonnet he is treating a variant of that earlier idea. The young man's appearance still promises love, though not his sexual potency but his sincerity is now in question; and this promise too is empty, a pledge which he will not redeem.

These two poems are followed by one of the crucial sonnets of the sequence, whose importance is signalled by an unexpected change of idiom from plaintive to magisterial. Sonnet 94 is by any critical standards a challenging poem; and in its proper

163

context it has the added force of a deeply considered commentary on issues which have been debated from the beginning of the sequence. Although it mentions neither the poet nor his friend, its relevance is not in doubt; for it sums up what the poet might have learnt from his perplexing experience in a statement which defines the friend's character with absolute and damning finality. Its masterly summing-up constitutes an imaginative terminus of the Sonnets: a point where concepts which Shakespeare has been struggling to reduce to intelligible order lock into place and cease to trouble him. In its impersonality and detachment the sonnet stands apart from the story; appropriately, for its resolution of ideas cannot be attributed to the poet who speaks almost every other sonnet, and its magisterial voice is not his. When he resumes the story in Sonnet 95, he is puzzled and hurt as before. Sonnet 94 has been subjected to a great deal of critical discussion; from which it follows that it has been very variously explained. In the main, disagreement over its meaning springs from uncertainty whether the sonnet is to be read as an unrelated, self-explanatory analysis of a particular type of person, or as the kind of imaginative summing-up already suggested. Those who take the second view will be ready, with Professor Knights, to recognise the ironic pretence of approval that gives bite to the delayed judgement of the opening sentence. Others, who expose themselves to that critic's rebuke as being 'quite deaf to variations of tone', will suppose that the approval is unequivocal and genuine:

> They that have power to hurt, and will do none,
> That do not do the thing they most do show;
> Who, moving others, are themselves as stone:
> Unmoved, cold, and to temptation slow,
> They rightly do inherit heaven's graces.

The emphasis of the passage falls squarely upon an idea of

withdrawal from life, of a disinclination to commit the self to any positive relationship or course of action. Such a person has power but declines to use it, refuses to put his potentialities to the test of practice, allows others to be drawn to him but offers no return of kindly feeling; remaining stonily impassive and aloof. Setting aside considerations of tone, the intentions of the passage are indicated clearly enough by the repeated disappointing of expectation which it both describes and induces in the reader. To read the line,

> That do not do the thing they most do show,

as an expression of moral approval, or to suppose that the deliberately weighted epithets of the fourth line are respectful, betrays critical limitations more serious than tone-deafness. The effect of these opening four lines might be described as freezing: a dispassionate, unhurried dissection of character which reveals step by step the meanness of spirit lying behind a mask of rectitude and abstinence. By holding back the main clause of his sentence until the fifth line, Shakespeare gives himself room to establish this quality of character firmly enough for his unexpected judgement to catch the reader off balance:

> They rightly do inherit heaven's graces.

If his ironic tone were not evident, the inconsistency of this conclusion with the picture of arid, ungenerous nature which it follows, and the bitter energy of the line, should reveal Shakespeare's purpose. A reader of the Sonnets who identifies the meanly retentive character described here will not need such prompting. Whether or not the poet is still speaking in Sonnet 94, the nature which is being dissected has not changed. The temperament that shows itself 'as stone' and unresponsive to temptation is more immediately akin to Adonis than to the friend; but both fall under the sonnet's indictment of those who will not put their energies to use, who refuse to do sexually 'the thing they most do show', and who excite desire or affection in others yet remain disdainfully unmoved themselves. The next line removes any lingering doubts about Shakespeare's intentions, and about the moral attitude which the sonnet carries forward. Those who inherit heaven's graces,

> And husband nature's riches from expense,

seem to be acting commendably; but only if the poem is read outside the context of ideas from which the Sonnets draw much of their meaning. Within this context, spending is habitually associated with the natural processes on which increase depends. Both Adonis and the young man are encouraged to be prodigal in spending themselves, and warned against the miserliness that denies nature the proper return of her openhanded liberality. In the world at large the husbandry of Sonnet 94, which is to prevent the spending of nature's riches, might be the mark of a good steward; but in the Sonnets it connotes unthriftiness and waste, the selfish hoarding of potential given to be expended. This moral position is defined by the group of poems from which the main argument of the sequence is evolved; and in the magisterial summing-up of Sonnet 94 its tenets are recalled in an ironic pretence of supporting the attitude which they expressly condemn. To assume with Beeching and Dover Wilson that the poet is protesting against those who impulsively 'squander their endowments' the reader must ignore the warning of Sonnet 9 that self-retentiveness is the enemy of the gift which the friend wishes to preserve for himself:

> And kept unused the user so destroys it.

The reader must also deny the imaginative integrity of the sequence, as a body of poetry bound together by persistent interests which fluctuate but do not radically change. Their persistence is proved again in the next two lines of Sonnet 94:

> They are the lords and owners of their faces,
> Others but stewards of their excellence.

Beeching goes wrong not only in failing to detect Shakespeare's irony, but in supposing that 'their excellence' relates not to those who are mere stewards without property of their own, but to the lords and owners of the previous line. Properly understood, the passage offers an antithesis between those who possess and those who manage or administer an estate, and involves the same metaphor of personal beauty in both. Shakespeare has returned to a concern of the early sonnets: the idea that nature's generous lending of gifts must be repaid through an equally liberal spending of personal energies, and that her loans must not be regarded as private possessions. When the poet speaks of the young man's good looks as 'the beauty which you hold in lease', he is trying to impress a sense of stewardship upon his friend, whose whole inclination is to claim the credit due to nature and to spend her rich gift upon himself. It is just this attitude which the poet now represents in a comment which sardonically inverts the standards consistently advanced in earlier sonnets, and whose ironic purpose leaves some readers facing in the wrong direction. The pattern of character which this sonnet discloses is in fact closely consistent with what has been observed piecemeal over the course of the poet's relationship with his friend, whose nature is now being expertly delineated. The person whose whole appearance is a lifeless sham, who makes no emotional communication with others, is identified by the self-love which makes him mistake his natural gifts for attributes of his own, and waste them in self-admiration. If the speaker had ever been deceived by such a person, he has learnt to recognise the signs of self-destructive imposture and to follow its now predictable workings. In their irony and impersonality his comments express the speaker's mastery of an enigma which formerly troubled and misled him. From being the victim of the young man's endlessly equivocal charm, he has become the unsparing analyst of his self-contradictory being.

This authority and psychological insight leave their final stamp upon the poem in the epigram which concludes it:

> Lilies that fester smell far worse than weeds.

The speaker is no longer ironic; for the underlying contempt of his commentary has risen to the surface in the language of open disgust—fester, smell, worse than weeds—which exposes the driving motive of the poem. This energy, like the absence of any explicit reference to the usual features of the story, is not accountable by an interpretation that makes Sonnet 94 part of an appeal or of a farewell address written to the poet's friend. Its drive comes from an imaginative pressure which can be explained only by showing its significance for Shakespeare, and not by treating his creatures as though they were capable of revealing their own purposes. The authoritative tone of the poem, so uncharacteristic of the poet's often plaintive or self-depreciatory mood, suggests that the long process of imaginative enquiry carried out through the Sonnets has come to a point of resolution. Like a man who has repeatedly submitted himself to the same obscure experience in order to understand it, Shakespeare has acquired the power of representing an obsessive imaginative figure in a form which accounts for it exactly and finally. He has detached himself from the ideas which he has been struggling to realise through the story of the poet's uncertain relationship with a miserly friend. In studying the contradictions of the friend's nature, and the starved creative potentiality that accompanies his self-love, the poet has been extending Shakespeare's awareness of creative power as a force

which may either liberate or wreck the personality of its owner.
Sonnet 94 indicates that this awareness has reached the stage at
which it can itself provide the impulse of a poem, and demonstrate what power is released with this widening of creative
consciousness.

M   169

CHAPTER SEVEN
Shakespeare's Dualism

DUALISM is a conspicuous feature of the complex experience which the Sonnets describe. In both sequences, the speaker is occupied with an attempt to form and ratify an association with a second person without whom he feels hungrily incomplete. Neither attempt is successful, and failure forces him to recognise his separateness from both friend and mistress, who frustrate his desire for close relationship by much the same indifference or evasiveness. In the second sequence the lover's inability to join himself with his mistress represents the form of a dualistic conflict within himself, as sense and judgement contradict one another by seeing her as both fascinating and repellent. Within the broader experience divided between the strongly contrasting figures of fair friend and ugly mistress, the speaker repeatedly alludes to contradictions in his own nature. His eye and heart

> are at a mortal war,
> How to divide the conquest of thy sight.
>   [46

He is prepared to bring accusations against himself on the friend's behalf [49]. He is attacked by contrary impulses which allow him no settled content:

> Now proud as an enjoyer, and anon
> Doubting the filching age will steal his treasure.
>   [75

When he is full of 'ne'er cloying sweetness' he perversely seeks out the opposite flavour:

To bitter sauces did I frame my feeding.

[118

In apologising to the friend whom he has betrayed, he admits that feelings have impelled him to act against his own vital interests, and to destroy what he most prized:

What wretched errors hath my heart committed,
Whilst it hath thought itself so blessed never?

[119

The friend is even more radically divided against himself. From the opening sonnets, which warn him against the consuming self-love that turns life inward upon itself, he is consistently shown to be a man in conflict with his own being and purposes. He commits 'murd'rous shame' upon himself, and has to be pardoned of 'self-doing crime' [9, 58]. He abuses the poet's trust by his seeming affection—'Thy looks with me, thy heart in other place' [93]—or by a natural duplicity which does not ruffle the disarming beauty of his appearance. He is the master-mistress of the poet's passion, having a woman's softness and charm but the genitalia of a man [20]. His doubleness of nature and character presents a problem to those poets who try to describe him, and those who can tell 'that you are you' will distinguish themselves [84]. This personal ambiguity extends to the poet's relationship with him, which in its rare moments of happiness allows the poet to exchange beings with the friend and to be a sharer in his attributes. 'Mine eyes have drawn thy shape,' he tells the friend,

and thine for me
Are windows to my breast, where-through the sun
Delights to peep, to gaze therein on thee.

[24

Their two personalities are so closely combined that the poet cannot praise his friend without flattering himself, as joint possessor of his beauty. ''Tis thee, myself,' he explains;

171

admitting that in this integration their two beings produce a contradictory figure, both itself and another. The association is not altogether to the poet's advantage, and he sometimes wishes to dissolve the partnership he has been so eager to form; as in Sonnet 39, where he proposes that they should live separately.

This characteristic motif of the Sonnets has been examined in earlier chapters of this book, and there is no need to enumerate its dualistic figures here. So tireless a theme, imprinted upon every possible element of the poet's story, is an idiom which reflects a particular imaginative interest not to be exhausted before the end of Shakespeare's career. It represents an integral part of the meaning of the Sonnets, in the same way as iterative images contribute to the whole sense of individual plays. Like them, it indicates an area of poetic attention whose topography Shakespeare maps out and reconsiders endlessly, varying his account of its features as he encounters fresh aspects of their nature. His great interest in the theme is implicit in the un-expectedly narrow scope of the whole poem, which limits its *dramatis personae* to three characters and permits only two to appear together. By linking the poet with a single friend, whether man or mistress, and showing little concern for the three-sided relationship which they sometimes contrive, Shakespeare concentrates attention upon the relationship of two people, and secures the conditions in which the motif of dualism can best be exploited. The restricted field of the Sonnets was probably determined by this purpose, which required the closed circle of an intimate personal relationship as its narrative basis. The dualistic associations which the poet forms constitute the heart of the sequence: imaginatively, they are what the whole poem is about.

Such a statement will not seem arbitrary to a reader who has already recognised how much of Shakespeare's early work is dominated by dualistic figures. The Sonnets have been so variously interpreted that any new reading has to fight to make itself heard; but the two narrative poems have aroused no such bitter conflict of opinion, and it is possible to consider their dualism in a calmer and more discerning attitude of mind. Once the possibility of Shakespeare's being an actor in the story becomes irrelevant, dualistic figures can be judged simply within an imaginative context, as they deserve. Critics of the narrative poems have not attempted to identify Tarquin or Venus with Shakespeare, and these characters can be analysed without raising the kind of objection which meets similar analysis of the main actors in the story of the Sonnets, who are imaginatively related to them. The speaker who urges the young man to marry finds a counterpart in Venus, who repeats his argument when she denies Adonis's right to withold himself from the cycle of creation, and reappears, grotesquely transformed, in the Tarquin who tries to terrify Lucrece into submitting to his lust. The common ground between the Sonnets and the narrative poems extends a good deal further than this. Like the Sonnets, both *Venus and Adonis* and *Lucrece* are closed poems which deal intensively with the relationships of two isolated characters, and allowing subsidiary figures a very minor place in the story. Only once in *Lucrece*, during the heroine's contemplation of the Troy picture, does the narrative open out and offer the kind of panoramic inclusiveness which characterises Shakespeare's dramatic outlook.

More significant, a frustrated attempt to bring about an integrated relationship between two characters forms the central theme of all three works. In the Sonnets, the poet's efforts to realise a permanent, closely familiar partnership with the friend repeatedly come to nothing, as do the lover's appeals to the Dark Lady. Adonis stubbornly refuses to yield to the arguments and physical inducements by which Venus tries to persuade him to make love. Lucrece resists Tarquin's appetite still more desperately, and although she is forced to yield to him, their sexual embrace is no union but a violation of her single self. Sexual passion is a motivating force in all but the first of these abortive relationships, though it figures in the Dark Lady sequence; but none of the poems seems to have been written with an erotic intention. Their common concern with sexual consummation is better explained by the powerful symbolic significance of the sexual act, as representing the integrating of separate persons in a single body. This is the attainment which the main character in each of Shakespeare's three poems strains after, and fails to achieve.

Unlike *Lucrece* and many of the sonnets, *Venus and Adonis* does not always treat dualism seriously. In the earlier of the two narrative poems Shakespeare seems to regard dualistic concepts mainly as a means of giving his story witty embellishment. When he makes Venus speak of nature 'with herself at strife' in creating Adonis, he skates over a topic whose depths he has still to discover. In the same playful spirit Venus describes Narcissus as a man who 'himself himself forsook', and warns Adonis that by not fathering a child he commits suicide:

> in thyself thyself art made away.

Evidently word-play holds more interest for Shakespeare than the state of self-conflict briefly revealed in Adonis, whose dualistic nature engages Shakespeare's fancy rather than his imagination. The figures which he develops from this theme are as yet flourishes on the surface of the story, not reflections of its inner meaning. Venus diagnoses the conflict in Adonis less picturesquely than she recalls her subjugation of Mars,

> Leading him prisoner in a red-rose chain,

but in a kindred image of paradoxical association. Herself and the unwilling Adonis form such another unlikely partnership of opposing temperaments:

> She red and hot as coals of glowing fire;
> He red for shame, but frosty in desire.

174

The playing on contrasts of heat and colour which continues throughout the poem has little serious significance or function beyond its decorative effect. Shakespeare is giving proof of his inventive wit by repeatedly drawing together unlike qualities into new and surprising relationships.

Yet the poem itself describes a failure to combine such antithetical figures. The kind of union which Shakespeare continually brings about in the verbal conceits of *Venus and Adonis* is denied to its human characters, who represent qualities as opposite as those married by his wit. The emphasis of the story falls upon differences of temperament that cannot be reconciled: upon a puritanical abstinence that snubs and checks all the arguments and physical advances of an eager fecundity; and upon a self-regard that perversely withdraws itself from life, refusing to spend its creative energies upon the purpose they were meant to serve. When Venus insists that Adonis is under a moral obligation to repay nature's loan, he rebuts her argument by maintaining that he is immature and so not ready for the task. Behind their fruitless contest of wills and bodies, his bare escape and her near-fulfilment, the mating of Adonis's horse with the jennet provides a silent and ironic comment on Venus's failure to arouse any excitement in his master. The incident suggests the deliberateness of Shakespeare's intention in writing a poem in which an almost frantic desire never achieves its expected fulfilment, and whose readers must share the frustrating experience of being cheated of a natural climax. It must seem odd that the first published work of so great a poet should have so negative a theme, and concern itself at such length with an impulse that remains obstructed and unsatisfied. The vigour and assurance of Shakespeare's style make this preoccupation with frustrated impulse still more difficult to understand. A major poet giving the first evidence of an abundant invention and fluency might have been expected to choose a dynamic, positive subject; but clearly Shakespeare was not interested merely in expressing his enjoyment of the creative power that is manifest in the copiousness of his writing. The parobolic flights of wit speak of his creative excitement clearly enough; but the story insists upon failure and frustration as a subject to which Shakespeare is imaginatively committed, whatever the success of the poem as a work of literary craftsmanship.

The dualistic features of *Venus and Adonis* are less marked than in *Lucrece* partly because the drive towards a fusion of opposites is expressed more violently in Tarquin than in Venus, and partly because in the earlier poem the characters are much less divided in themselves. Venus describes the self-conflict in Adonis in terms familiar from the opening group of sonnets, which were not necessarily written before the narrative poem. Her mocking account of the narcissism which dominates Adonis is a more vigorous form of the protest voiced by the poet against the young man's indifference to woman and married life:

> Is thine own heart to thine own face affected?
> Can thy right hand seize love upon thy left?
> Then woo thyself, be of thyself rejected;
> Steal thine own freedom, and complain on theft.
> > Narcissus so himself himself forsook,
> > And died to kiss his shadow in the brook.
>
> [157–162

Her mockery is a warning, not an analysis of Adonis's actual condition; though her later remarks about 'love-lacking vestals and self-loving nuns' suggest that Venus diagnoses this fault in Adonis. By refusing to leave children to posterity, she tells him, he is in effect committing suicide:

> So in thyself thyself art made away;
> A mischief worse than civil home-bred strife,
> Or theirs whose desperate hands themselves do slay.
>
> [763–765

As the most emphatic expression of self-conflict, suicide holds an interest for Shakespeare which is displayed more fully in *Lucrece*. Here it is introduced only as a talking-point, and does not become an issue of the story. Like the suggestion that Adonis is involved in a narcissistic relationship with himself, the idea is presented more as a witty fancy than as the serious imaginative concept which it later becomes. The division which might allow one half of Adonis's personality to woo the other, and be rejected by it, is a notion indulgently treated as yet; and is too lightly stressed for Adonis to appear as a developed figure of self-conflict.

The subject of *Lucrece* does not invite such treatment; but Shakespeare may have chosen this darker theme because it allowed him to exploit an interest in dualism which had grown rapidly since the writing of *Venus and Adonis*. From its opening stanzas, *Lucrece* suggests that Shakespeare has become aware of an imaginative depth in the ideas of his earlier poem. Where the variation between red and white in Venus's face has only a decorative purpose, extended to Adonis and even to the boar, in Lucrece 'this silent war of lilies and of roses' is described with a particularity that implies appreciation of the personal conflict which it symbolises. The heroine is presented from the outset as a woman of divided impulse,

> Within whose face beauty and virtue strived
> Which of them both should underprop her fame;
>
> [52–3

in whom 'beauty's red and virtue's white' are constantly at war, impelled by the same ambitious desire to usurp the other's place:

> The sov'reignty of either being so great
> That oft they interchange each other's seat.
>
> [69–70

The account of this civil war in Lucrece's complexion is as decorative and witty as anything in *Venus and Adonis*; but the military images of the passage–shield, fight, war, ranks, vanquished, armies, yield, triumph–forcibly underline her associations with self-conflict. For the moment this characteristic exists only in the conceit by which the story pays tribute to Lucrece's modesty and charm; but the passage gives proof of a strong imaginative interest already searching for expression, which later in the poem is realised in physical terms.

In Tarquin Shakespeare finds a figure whose dualism is at once plausible. The warring white and red that make Lucrece seem a creature of conflicting impulses do not represent her moral character; but Tarquin is both a moral contradiction, 'whose inward ill no outward harm expressed', and a man at war with himself. To achieve his evil purpose, he has first to overcome his own repugnance and to silence the desperate arguments of his better self, which recognises the lasting dishonour he must bring upon his name by violating his hostess. If he is to rape Lucrece, he must first do violence upon himself, by outraging the moral principles that are as much a part of him as his sexual appetite. In this way, when he violates Lucrece he enacts the overwhelming of conscience by animal impulse within his moral being which has allowed him to attack her. As Lucrece pleads desperately against his brutal intention, she is repeating the protests which his own moral sense has already uttered. To this extent Lucrece identifies herself with the voice of moral protest which Tarquin silences before he enters her bedchamber: like it, she is to be muffled by her attacker, and prevented from crying out. While remaining in the fullest sense a character in the story, Lucrece acquires a very powerful imaginative significance; and, exploiting the double identity which she assumes, Shakespeare is able to make one account describe both the rape of Lucrece and Tarquin's outraging of his own moral being.

The imaginative seriousness of what is represented by the rape of Lucrece should make us ready to see a good deal more than rhetorical ingenuity in Tarquin's debate with himself; for the moral conflict which he undergoes before he reaches his decision, 'madly tossed between desire and dread,' is not a studied prologue devised to delay the climax of Shakespeare's narrative, but a vital preliminary to what follows. When he rapes Lucrece, Tarquin is overthrown by the force within himself which is seen warring with his respect for decency and good name. His debate with himself includes its share of the verbal conceits which characterise Shakespeare's early writing. If Tarquin is to satisfy his lust, 'for himself himself he must forsake', like Narcissus in a very different situation; and where will he find truth

> if there be no self-trust?
> When shall he think to find a stranger just,
> When he himself himself confounds, betrays?
> [158–160

But although word-play persists, it is now accompanied by a graver appreciation of what such witty figures may signify. The iterative phrase 'himself himself' may be admitted partly as an aural conceit; but the imaginative scrutiny which dualistic concepts receive in this poem makes it seem more likely that the phrase represents Shakespeare's awareness of self-conflict. One himself reflects the other, but is a different self; and their likeness is too close for distinction. Each claims the authority due to the single self, and advances its own argument. Tarquin's judgement stands as arbiter between the contestants, 'frozen conscience and hot-burning will', which urge him towards opposite ends. He does not resolve this conflict within himself when he allows lust to control him; and when he answers Lucrece's appeal by telling her that he has already rejected the protests of his own conscience, he shows that despite the intensity of his desire his mind is acutely conscious of the moral perversity of what he is doing. There is no blotting-out of

179

reason, for it continues to warn Tarquin what terrible consequences must ensue while his animal appetite insists upon gratifying itself. 'I have debated even in my soul,' he tells Lucrece,
summarising the clash of purposes which he has now determined,

> 'What wrong, what shame, what sorrow I shall breed;
> But nothing can affection's course control,
> Or stop the headlong fury of his speed.
> I know repentant tears ensue the deed,
>   Reproach, disdain and deadly enmity;
>   Yet strive I to embrace mine infamy.'

[499–504

Tarquin could not recognise more lucidly that he proposes to
ruin himself. Although about to behave like a frenzied animal,
he continues to possess the moral awareness of a reasoning
being, whose lust must force its will upon his helpless judgement. He is entangled in his own cross-purposes, yet detached
enough from the conflict to describe the mad perversity of his
behaviour: 'yet strive I to embrace mine infamy.' The verb
gives the line a sense of straining energy which enforces the
impression of a personality divided against itself.

The rape which follows enacts the conflict within the single
being whose driving impulses work against one another.
Lucrece refuses to surrender to Tarquin's threat to murder and
defame her if she resists him; and the sexual act which she is
compelled to commit with him forces a brutal travesty of union
upon a completely un-cooperating victim. Their two beings
are not fused together in a mutual exchange of selves: there is
no integration, no meaningful partnership, and each remains
single and unrelated to the other. The emptiness of Tarquin's
achievement shows itself in the revulsion of feeling that succeeds
it. He has spent himself uselessly, without profit or enjoyment;
and, no less than Lucrece, he suffers shame and disgust in his
failure:

He like a thievish dog creeps sadly thence,
She like a wearied lamb lies panting there;
He scowls and hates himself for his offence,
She desperate with her nails her flesh doth tear.

[736–9

The description of Tarquin's feelings after his crime renew the
early suggestions that the rape has a counterpart in the deadly
injury he inflicts upon himself. Like Lucrece, his own spiritual
being knows itself violated and defamed: a correspondence
made more pointed by the metaphor which makes Tarquin's
soul 'the spotted princess' whose temple has been desecrated
by his sin. This figurative being is sufficiently like Lucrece to
be mistaken for her even before she describes the injury which
she has suffered at Tarquin's hands:

She says her subjects with foul insurrection
Have battered down her consecrated wall,
And by their mortal fault brought in subjection
Her immortality, and made her thrall
To living death and pain perpetual.

[722–6

Lucrece herself might be speaking. The image of an enemy
battering down a wall is almost explicitly sexual, and the passage
foreshadows her own complaint against the pollution which
makes further life unthinkable. The ambiguity seems deliberate: the voice of Tarquin's outraged conscience cannot be
distinguished from the protest of the violated Lucrece, evidently because Shakespeare has seen one in terms of the other.
The two figures are associated in the image of 'foul insurrection', or civil war, which is central to the poem. The immediate sense of the passage makes us see Tarquin as a man
who has attacked the citadel of his own spiritual being, and
carried it by assault. Implicitly, the parallel with Lucrece
suggests that the rape stands in the relation of dramatic metaphor

to this conflict of individual will and judgement, where the 'spotted princess' is both Tarquin's soul and the woman whom he defiles. Her refusal to accept him, and his outraging of her chastity, give physical expression to the war within the divided personality of Tarquin which, imaginatively, is as much Shakespeare's subject as the rape of Lucrece.

Tarquin's part in the story ends when he leaves the bed-chamber, some eleven hundred lines before the conclusion of the poem. His departure at this point means that for the greater part of the poem Lucrece is its only effective figure, and that the narrative is more concerned with the sequel to the rape than with its preliminaries or the crime itself. This preponder-ance of interest is not perhaps entirely explained by the moral ambiguousness of Lucrece after her violation; but the changed character that she admits in herself gives Shakespeare a theme which he develops with a good deal of purpose. Hitherto his preoccupation with self-conflict has been expressed through Tarquin. At Tarquin's departure this interest is transferred to his victim, who 'bears the load of lust he left behind', and who feels herself deeply contaminated by the loathsome act to which she has submitted. There may be some encouragement to see Lucrece's self-condemnation directed against an un-acknowledged desire for Tarquin which has silently opposed her entirely virtuous denial of his suit. She resists him, but submits; and later she reflects that if she now seeks to kill herself in shame, she cannot argue that she was terrified into submission by Tarquin's threatening sword:

> I feared by Tarquin's falchion to be slain,
> Yet for the self-same purpose seek a knife.
> [1046–7

If Shakespeare intended her comment to be taken in this sense, his disclosure of an unrecognised motive in Lucrece cannot have been meant to bring her essentially virtuous character into question. The ambivalence which she discovers in herself is a condition of the poem rather than of her psychology; and in submitting to Tarquin to avoid being killed, yet committing suicide in her dishonour, Lucrece acts by contradictory standards that are deeply implanted in the poem. Rape transforms her into a morally ambiguous figure, still virtuous in her mind but indelibly corrupted by Tarquin's lust. Like him she has suffered an assault which has degraded her body, the physical partner of her innocent soul, beyond hope of recovery:

> Her house is sacked, her quiet interrupted,
> Her mansion battered by the enemy;
> Her sacred temple spotted, spoiled, corrupted,
> Grossly engirt with daring infamy.
>
> [1170–73

The verbal parallel between this passage and lines 722–6 draws Lucrece and Tarquin together, inviting us to see them rather as related forms of the same being than as wrongdoer and victim. Lucrece has not done violence to the integrity of her inner self, as Tarquin by submitting to lustful impulse; but in the sense that she too has given way before an assault of blind appetite Lucrece has duplicated his crime, and has involved herself in the same defilement. Imaginatively, she becomes Tarquin by giving voice to the profound spiritual distress which he feels in his physical bestialism. Her disgust and self-hatred extend the tortured feelings which Tarquin has already experienced, in the helpless wish of the inner self to be dissociated from the contaminated partner to whom it is bound, and whose disgrace it must share. Although physically stained, she insists that her mind is still immaculate; and by speaking of this virtuous spirit, which, 'still pure,'

> Doth in her poisoned closet yet endure,
>
> [1659

she suggests the oppression of the self that is trapped within a morally loathsome body.

The dichotomy which makes of Lucrece two incompatible selves is represented in the debate which she carries on with herself before Collatine's arrival, and in the self-destructive act of suicide which ends the story. Her debate is the counterpart of Tarquin's argument between the conflicting impulses of lust and moral restraint earlier in the poem. Like him, she will choose a course which injures her irremediably; but before she reaches this decision, Lucrece like Tarquin finds herself caught in a moral conflict too severe to be quickly resolved. She too is a being painfully divided against herself:

> [As] one encompassed with a winding maze,
> That cannot tread the way out readily,
> So with herself is she in mutiny.
>
> [1151–53

The prospect of suicide raises further divided issues. Itself a mortal sin, it would add spiritual damnation to the defilement which her body has suffered:

> 'To kill myself,' quoth she, 'alack, what were it
> But with my body my poor soul's pollution?'
>
> [1156–57

On the other hand, if she is now to take her life to wipe out the stain which her body has received, she will be showing an undue preference for one part of herself, where previously she felt a natural regard for each:

> 'My body or my soul, which was the dearer
> When the one pure the other made divine?
> Whose love of either to myself was nearer
> When both were kept for heaven and Collatine?'
>
> [1163–66

Even here indecision is implicit; for although Lucrece is ostensibly describing a state of personal integration, her questions suggest that she is trying to determine a preference where her feelings were too nicely poised to make a clear choice possible. The fact that this is no longer the case throws her self-conflict into relief: her body is now 'this blemished fort', and she is so far from feeling love for it that she wishes to dissociate herself from it irrevocably, by striking herself dead. Her wish involves a paradox which rests upon the poem's crucial idea of personality at war with itself. The self from which Lucrece wants to be dissociated is not a separable part of her being, but a vital condition of her existence; and if she strikes this now hateful part of herself dead, the innocent must suffer with the guilty. Her suicide will be both an extreme manifestation of individuality divided against itself, and a proof of the interdependence of body and soul which Lucrece wishes to deny. It is not the soul which acts as executioner: the body must grasp and direct the knife which it drives into itself.

When she commits suicide Lucrece contrives to obscure this fact, and to present her action as though it were carried out by another person. Her last words identify Tarquin not as a rapist but as the assassin whose arm now strikes her dead; and she falls as victim of his murderous blow:

> Here with a sigh as if her heart would break,
> She throws forth Tarquin's name: 'He, he,' she says;
> But more than 'he' her poor heart could not speak,
> Till after many accents and delays,
> Untimely breathings, sick and short assays,
>   She utters this: 'He, he, fair lords, 'tis he
>   That guides this hand to give this wound to me.'
>   [1716–22

The conceit has a certain imaginative justice; for after the rape Lucrece is no longer her single self, but a contradictory mixture of personalities, herself and Tarquin at once. The defilement which he has implanted in her, and which she feels so alien to herself, is a new element of personality which Lucrece finds loathsome and wishes to destroy; but her pollution is part of the new self whom she has become. She has therefore some right to enact Tarquin, who is no longer a person distinct from herself; and to present her suicide as a murder carried out by the polluted Tarquin upon the chaste Lucrece, fusing both characters within her own ambiguous being. The laboured preliminaries to this symbolic splitting of personality suggest that Lucrece is making a supreme effort to separate the conflicting identities within herself in just this way. The outcome is a triumphant repudiation of her dishonoured self by the chaste Lucrece who now is only part of the flawed being she has become; but in repudiating her repulsive *alter ego* Lucrece proves her identity with it, for the same knife-thrust is fatal to both.

In acting-out her dualism through suicide, Lucrece foreshadows a later and more tragic figure of the plays. However much unlike Othello in other respects, she and the Moor are closely akin in their common refusal to acknowledge themselves in the irretrievably dishonoured beings which they become, and in their determination to sever themselves from a shameful counterpart. Like Lucrece, Othello makes his suicide look like an attack upon a second figure who, in fact, is another aspect of himself—the malignant Turk of his reminiscence. When he strikes down this evil figure at the end of his anecdote, Othello restores his noble identity, reliving his triumph at Aleppo and demonstrating his separateness from the devilish being who has taken possession of him. Again like Lucrece, he enacts a commentary that is both true and false. He is simultaneously the noble servant of the state and its detestable enemy; and when he acts the part of avenging justice he must also represent its victim, and fall as the hated Turk whom his poniard stabs. His actions are insistently equivocal, as this attempt to disguise suicide reveals; and the dualism which he betrays by dividing himself between heroic type and depraved antitype, one executing the other as a manifestation of his nobility, dominates his character. The shock of discovering his bestial self presents a challenge to Othello's conception of himself which he cannot absorb. He can only resolve the contradiction between self and self by violently dissociating himself from his degraded counterpart; but the blow which severs them ends the life of his noble self, and proves their single identity.

The dualistic figures which are so imaginatively potent in *Lucrece*, and which seem to have determined the general shape of both narrative poems, have the persistence of a major preoccupation extending well beyond Shakespeare's early work. This is not the place to follow the development of so vigorous an interest, whose energies are still running strongly in *The Tempest*; but rather to indicate how the plays of the period probably covered by the Sonnets are affected by the same dominant concern with self-conflict. Between *Lucrece* and the first of Shakespeare's plays the imaginative gulf is very wide, and it may seem unlikely that a poem involving only two characters, or a single figure of divided identity, should share much ground with history-plays as humanly comprehensive as the three parts of *Henry VI*. But the major concern of Shakespeare's history-plays is civil war, which is self-conflict on a national scale. In the closing speech of *Richard III* the new king sums up the years of political unrest as a madness which has induced England to do violence upon herself, and made unity impossible in the family as in the state:

> England hath long been mad, and scarred herself;
> The brother blindly shed the brother's blood,
> The father rashly slaughtered his own son,
> The son compelled been butcher to the sire:
> All this divided York and Lancaster
> Divided, in their dire division.

[v.5. 23–8

Speeches of this kind are conventionally read as moral injunc-
tions by Shakespeare against disrespect for the authority which
upholds the ordered harmony of government; but we may
doubt whether their imaginative significance lies quite so close
to their literal meaning. If we suppose that Shakespeare is
developing his interest in dualism by following the growth of
self-conflict within the body politic, we shall find supporting
evidence in the behaviour of some of his major characters in
these plays, who epitomise the same condition in their individual selves. Under Richard III, England reflects the self-
hatred of the usurper, who describes the turmoil of conflicting
purposes which drive him towards his ambition:

> Seeking a way, and straying from the way,
> Not knowing how to find the open air,
> But toiling desperately to find it out,
> Torment myself to catch the English crown.
> [*Hen.VI. 3;* iii. 2. 177–180

When he starts out of his nightmare before his last battle he
reveals more fully the disorganised personality in which every
impulse of thought or feeling is immediately countered by its
opposite, and the self feels its existence threatened by its own
hostile energies. Shakespeare is translating the leisurely narrative
account of Lucrece's contradictory purposes into dramatic
speech:

> What, do I fear myself? There's none else by:
> Richard loves Richard; that is, I am I.
> Is there a murderer here? No: yes, I am.
> Then fly! What, from myself? great reason, why?
> Lest I revenge. What, myself upon myself?
> Alack, I love myself. Wherefore? for any good
> That I myself have done unto myself?
> O no: alas, I rather hate myself
> For hateful deeds committed by myself.

I am a villain: yet I lie, I am not.
Fool, of thyself speak well: fool, do not flatter.
[*Richard III.* v.3. 182–192

The translation is jerky and awkward, and contains no single
striking expression of the idea which Richard is fumbling with;
but Shakespeare is clearly pursing the same interest as makes
Lucrece turn upon herself. Richard begins by asserting the
singleness of his personality, 'I am I'; though prefacing this
with a remark which admits his self-love and so hints at a
narcissistic relationship, which must involve duplicity in two
senses of the term. The recognition that he is in the presence of
a murderer awakes an impulse of fear which he immediately
dismisses as absurd: 'myself upon myself' is a dualistic formula
too paradoxical for his reason to accept, though it is by reasoning that he discovers his contradictory feelings towards himself.
It is a weakness of his soliloquy that it works out his dualism
logically, and without the apparent contradictions of sense that
give Lucrece's promise,

Myself, thy friend, will kill myself, thy foe
[1196

the convincing quality of a mind divided between opposite
and incompatible judgements of itself. But to question the
effectiveness of Richard's speech does not reduce the imaginative significance of its interest in conflict within the personality,
whose fully expanded form is represented by the civil wars
which provide a major theme of Shakespeare's early work.

The comedies present the same subject in the domestic
context of marriage and friendship. The twin brothers of the
Menaechmi made a predictable appeal to Shakespeare's developing recognition of dualism by offering him figures with obvious
comic potentialities through whom he could work out this
imaginative interest, sometimes with more serious purpose

than the dramatic situation suggests. When Adriana mistakes
the second Antipholus for her husband she brings about a richly
comic state of affairs; but her attempts to understand his distant
attitude include some comments on marriage which impinge
directly upon the subject of personal integration. 'How comes
it', she asks,

> That thou art then estranged from thyself?
> Thyself I call it, being strange to me,
> That undividable, incorporate,
> Am better than thy dear self's better part.
> [*Errors*, ii. 2. 120–3

The ideas underlying her argument are not at all comic.
Adriana is claiming that, as a wife, she is an incorporate part of
the single body formed by her husband and herself; and
insisting that by treating her as a stranger Antipholus alienates
himself from his own being. Pursuing her argument, she
asserts that because they are one flesh she must share the dishonour of any crime committed by her husband. Her speech
is comic only because it is addressed to the wrong Antipholus,
who does not know what to make of her appeal: what she says
has an imaginative importance as great as the self-loathing of
Lucrece in her defilement, which the speech brings to mind:

> I am possessed with an adulterate blot,
> My blood is mingled with the crime of lust;
> For if we two be one, and thou play false,
> I do digest the poison of thy flesh,
> Being strumpeted by thy contagion.
> [ii. 2. 140–4

The New Arden editor regards Adriana's desire for identity
with her husband as evidence of a jealous and possessive nature;
but we are not obliged to judge her behaviour by the standards
of everday life. Her argument is shaped by an imaginative

purpose that links together the poems and the early plays; and when she claims to share a single being with her husband, Adriana is not so much revealing her dramatic character as allowing Shakespeare to realise an obsessive theme of his work. Here she is made to speak like Lucrece in reverse; for where Lucrece is horrified by being incorporated with Tarquin's lust, Adriana seems eager to affirm the guilt which springs from her common identity with Antipholus. The difference is simply accountable in the fact that Tarquin is not husband to Lucrece; but both women can be innocently 'strumpeted by contagion', whether taken lawfully or not. It would be mistaken to infer any moral intention on Shakespeare's part from such speeches, as it is to read character into them. Their significance is essentially imaginative; and their ideas are directed by the poet's interest in contrary natures or states of being which merge or fuse together, to produce an ambivalent figure divided against itself.

In Shakespeare's second comedy, which has no married characters, his main figures are bound together by ties of friendship and love; and it is within these relationships that he presents the paradox of shared personality. If the friendship of Valentine and Proteus seems implausibly close, we may have to make allowance for an imaginative need on Shakespeare's part to describe a relationship so familiar that each character may speak of himself as though he were the other. We should not dismiss Valentine's claim to know Proteus 'as myself' as hyperbolic, nor see only clowning in the confusions of Launce's demonstration:

> This hat is Nan our maid, I am the dog: no, the dog is himself, and I am the dog: O the dog is me, and I am myself.
> *Two Gentlemen* ii.3. 23–5

The hyperbole and the nonsense are alike determined by an imaginative condition of the play, which treats not simply of

THE MASTER-MISTRESS

identity but the doubling of self with a single personality. As in other plays, such doubleness involves duplicity; and two of the bifold characters produced by deep affection revolt against themselves in the course of the action. The more obvious of them is Proteus, who recognises that to woo Silvia he must be false to his second self Valentine and to his own mistress Julia. When he concludes,

> I cannot now prove constant to myself
> Without some treachery used to Valentine,
> > ii. 6. 31–2

he ignores the force of his relationship with Valentine, which binds them into one composite being. In the sense that Valentine is 'myself' to Proteus, his remark contradicts itself by equating loyalty 'to myself' with treachery towards a second figure who is not distinct from himself. The two halves of this composite personality are in conflict. The same contradictions appear in his neatly argued proof that to betray his friend and his mistress will be to his advantage:

> If I keep them, I needs must lose myself;
> If I lose them, thus find I by their loss:
> For Valentine, myself: for Julia, Silvia.
> I to myself am dearer than a friend.
> > ii. 6 20–3

Proteus cannot lose himself by keeping Valentine's friendship, since his friend is himself; and what is true of the friend in Sonnet 16–'to give yourself away keeps yourself still'–applies to Proteus in another sense. Again, there can be no such exchange as he proposes, 'for Valentine, myself', since their friendship incorporates them. The common identity which their relationship gives them invalidates the selfish comment, 'I to myself am dearer than a friend', by proving its deeper truth: to the 'myself' who is Valentine, Proteus is indeed dearer

192

than a friend; and for this reason his impulse to betray Valentine is perversely self-injuring.

Unlike Proteus, Julia acts against her private interests knowingly, out of love for the man who is betraying her trust. In the character of Sebastian she becomes the first of Shakespeare's heroines who make themselves sexually equivocal by adopting male attire: outwardly a man, she has the feelings and constitution of a woman. Like Rosalind and Viola, she enriches the play by the comedy and pathos of her situation; and like them in her curious blend of male and female attributes she seems to represent the paradox of a personality at odds with itself, that is so dominant a figure of Shakespeare's imaginative outlook. As Sebastian, Julia accepts the further ambiguity of undertaking services for Proteus which in her own identity she could not carry out:

> To plead for that which I would not obtain,
> To carry that which I would have refused,
> To praise his faith, which I would have dispraised.
> [iv. 4. 105–7

Her assumed character is in conflict with the womanly self of which it is part; but unlike Proteus she resolves her dilemma by betraying her private interests instead of mistakenly trying to protect them at her lover's expense. Her decision is in pointed contrast with Proteus's plot against his friend Valentine; but like that, it involves an act of treachery which must be damaging to the actor. Perhaps because her love is greater, Julia recognises this:

> I am my master's true confirmed love;
> But cannot be true servant to my master
> Unless I prove false traitor to myself.
> [iv. 4. 108–10

This 'myself' is a more certain identity than the inconstant Proteus possesses; but in her conversation with Silvia, Julia makes her self appear a more divided figure than her constancy suggests. Personating Sebastian and speaking about the deserted Julia, she creates an illusion of a second being whom she knows 'almost as well as I do know myself', who is 'as black as I' and 'about my stature'; a Julia very much like herself, though not entirely identical with her. The figment of a double-Julia is supported by a second phantasmal figure who is her counterpart in everything but sex. In the Pentecost play which she describes to Silvia,

> I was trimmed in Madam Julia's gown,
> Which served me as fit, by all men's judgements,
> As if the garment had been made for me;
> Therefore I know she is about my height.
>
> [iv. 4. 166–9

While Julia is actually wearing Sebastian's clothes, Sebastian is speaking of the occasion when he wore her gown. In terms of story there is no real ambiguity here: Sebastian is an imposture, and the gown which fitted 'him' was in fact being worn by Julia. The imaginative implications of her story are less easily disposed of. It seems that Sebastian and Julia are aspects of a single personality which are sufficiently alike to be inter-changeable: that she is speaking through him, as on a previous occasion he spoke through her; and that each dresses in the other's clothes, which fit the same body. The suggested reversal of Julia's transvestism in the male figure which she assumes is amusingly contrived; but the conceit has an entirely serious association with the motif of dualism represented by the term 'master-mistress'. As Julia continues her story, she develops the idea of her divided nature in another direction. Still speaking as Sebastian, and explaining what a pathetic role she had acted–'Ariadne, passioning for Theseus's perjury'– Julia tells Silvia how this woeful performance had moved her mistress to tears:

I so lively acted with my tears
That my poor mistress, moved therewithal,
Wept bitterly; and would I might be dead
If I in thought felt not her very sorrow.

[iv. 4. 174-7

Sebastian's 'poor mistress' is of course Julia herself, who is now claiming to have been both actor and audience; though the part of Ariadne is clearly a means of expressing her grief over her betrayal by Proteus, which had not happened at the time of the supposed play. At this point the actual circumstances of Julia's story become impossible to make out; for if she was the actor-actress who wore Julia's gown she could not also have been the spectator who wept at Sebastian's performance. In asserting, through Sebastian, that she felt the same grief as the spectator Julia, she is tacitly admitting that he and she are the same person; but at the level of literal interpretation this makes her story pointless, for why should Julia go to such lengths to persuade Silvia that she was moved to tears by a play? The passage is obviously to be taken in an imaginative sense; and some part of its purpose must be to associate Julia with Ariadne's grief yet to detach her from it, and then again to involve her emotionally. As Sebastian, she enacts Ariadne with simulated tears and arouses genuine compassion in the spectator Julia, who weeps at the performance. This spectacle of true grief is then reflected back to the actor Sebastian, who feels the 'very sorrow' which his acting has evoked, and responds like a spectator to the no less 'lively' enacting of Julia's grief. Since in fact Julia and Sebastian are the same person, no such process of enacting and responding could have occurred; but it is none the less described, and in an imaginative sense it happens. Julia's male counterpart, disguised in her clothes, plays Ariadne to her; and in her distress she re-enacts his performance, with Sebastian as deeply moved spectator. Each is the other, and both are herself. Unless we regard her story as an elaborate

195

attempt to hoodwink Silvia for no practical reason, the purpose
of the speech must lie in its imaginative significance. More than
one point is involved: unlike the stony-hearted Crab, who
refuses to shed a tear at his master's leave-taking, Julia is
generously compassionate; and even when she is simulating
grief she can be genuinely moved by another's tears. The main
significance of her speech lies elsewhere. It reveals a personality
divided between two selves that are linked in a complex
relationship; a being in whom male and female attributes are
both present, and of whom each part is capable of acting as
spectator to the other, and of sharing very largely in the other's
experience. To recognise the nature of this paradoxical being
does not help to explain Julia as a character; but it does throw
light upon the nature of the dualistic relationships to which
Shakespeare's imagination was giving form.

These typical passages of the poems and early plays provide
evidence of a concern with dualism and self-conflict that is not
confined to a single period of Shakespeare's work, or to a
particular kind of writing. We might judge from *Lucrece* that
Shakespeare's imagination was already deeply committed to
this subject, and that it was capable of acting upon his creative
purposes to the extent of determining both the narrative form
of the poem, the individual character of its actors, and the
nature of its crucial events. It would be strange if so powerful
an impulse of his poetry had left no mark on the Sonnets,
which belong to the same period. In fact they are more per-
sistently concerned with dualistic relationships than any other
of Shakespeare's works. It has already been suggested that this
is their central subject, and that the whole sequence represents
a tireless imaginative interrogation of the divided being whose
elements the poet longs to unify. With no obligation to divert
part of his energy to developing a story, Shakespeare was free
to concentrate upon the dualistic relationship of two figures,
which in the plays and narrative poems can be treated only

occasionally. The two figures are not always those of the poet
and his attractive friend. At the beginning of the sequence the
poet acts as commentator upon the divided state of the young
man, whose wilful behaviour proves him both in love with
himself–'contracted to thine own bright eyes'–and his own
enemy, intent upon destroying himself. Variations of this
theme occupy Shakespeare up to the point where this dualistic
relationship within the friend's personality is widened, to
involve two figures within the same kind of conflicting association, both affectionate and contemptuous. It is at this point, in
a literal interpretation of the Sonnets, that Shakespeare falls in
love with his noble friend, and begins to experience the mixture
of rapture and anguish that accompanies the continual fluctuations of the friend's regard. With an appreciation of Shakespeare's commitment to dualism as an imaginative theme, it
should be possible to form a more balanced view of what these
poems signify. Shakespeare is treating the same imaginative
subject as he develops in *Lucrece* and the plays cursorily considered above, but in a different manner. The ideas are presented in the form of a more or less continuous commentary
upon the progress of the relationship which the speaker is
trying to resolve between himself and a second being who is 'all
the better part of me': a half-private chronicle in which the
speaker is alone audible, and the second figure mistily indefinite.
Whether friend or mistress, the poet's companion is seldom
more than a notional presence: 'we never catch their profile, or
realise any single definite trait or act of theirs.'[1] Where the plays
and narrative poems attach Shakespeare's dualistic concepts to
firmly realised characters, the Sonnets make little attempt to
build up such impressions of personality, and concentrate upon
working-out the ideas that are their driving impulse.

In the opening group of sonnets dualism takes two main
forms, which together account for most of the poet's advice

[1] C. H. Herford *Works of Shakespeare,* London 1899; x.384.

to his unresponsive friend. The more obvious is expressed in the repeated warnings against the self-destructive impulse that leads the friend to commit 'murderous shame' upon himself. His crime is a refusal to marry and beget children, which the poet describes more fancifully as an unwillingness to make 'another self'. If Shakespeare's dualism is a serious imaginative concern, this apparently playful idea deserves to be studied attentively. While on one hand the friend is warned against the harm which his divided self may inflict upon his being, on the other he is encouraged to avoid singleness by creating a second figure of himself. The literal meaning of these sonnets, and their straightforward interest in marriage and sexual reproduction, are now seen as the outer husk of an imaginative purpose; a simple fictional situation contrived to allow Shakespeare to develop this major poetic motif. The sense of seemingly plain terms is deepened by the poetic intention which sets them in metaphorical association with its own far more complex concerns. When the poet enjoins his friend to leave behind 'some form' of himself, or cautions him

> Thou single wilt prove none
> [8

Shakespeare is using his fictional situation as the basis of an imaginative enquiry in which marriage and children have only a figurative importance, and whose centre lies in the enigmatic relationships that exist within the personality. The full sense of the cryptic comment, 'Thou single wilt prove none'–in part conceit, and in lesser part a detail of the fictional story–is to be understood within the context of the enquiry which is maintained throughout the Sonnets, and extends over the adjoining areas of Shakespeare's work. Its interests are not primarily psychological; for although Shakespeare seems to be discovering for himself the complex nature of human personality, he reaches no settled conclusions but develops his position continuously. If he appears to suggest in Sonnet 8 that a state of undivided personality is impossible, or equivalent to nonentity, we should not interpret the remark as an affirmation about the psychological nature of man. It reveals part of an imaginative attitude which no section of Shakespeare's work displays completely, and which never crystallises firmly enough to be defined. The critic must snatch up understanding on the march. The friend must not remain single, for in this state he cannot survive; nor must he destroy himself by conflict between the selves of a divided personality. This paradox represents the imaginative position from which the Sonnets begin to work out the more involved situations reached later in the sequence.

As a group, the marriage-sonnets define the seminal interests which the later poems continue to explore despite a change of subject-matter. The poet is not yet seriously involved with the young man–as some critics would have it, Shakespeare has not yet fallen in love with his noble patron; and his main concern is that the friend should duplicate himself. If these sonnets have any urgency of feeling, it is directed towards the need to form a second image of the friend: to 'breed another thee' who will be 'much liker than your painted counterfeit'. The poet's appeal for a close relationship with the friend comes later. For the moment the main focus of attention falls upon the idea of preserving the self by spending it,

> To give away yourself, keeps your self still;
>
> [16

where the generosity of love recreates all that it spends of itself; and upon a related idea of reproducing the form of the lover:

> Then you were
> Yourself again after your self's decease,
> When your sweet issue your sweet form should bear.
>
> [13

The proposal contains ambiguities which have already been noticed. The friend may choose to create either a genuine counterpart of himself in a son, or an admiring image returned by a mirror, having the form without the substance of true being. In either case he will enter a partnership with a second self, like him in all appearances and in kind; for if he does not create a child of flesh and blood but a shadow-figure the friend will lose his own substance as he becomes immersed in the mirror-world of his narcissism. In the marriage-sonnets the poet stands outside this projected association of twin selves, as a well-intentioned but disengaged third person urging the friend to realise the partnership which he describes. The break in the sequence occurs where the poet takes over the role of identical partner to the friend, and begins to describe such a relationship from within. Nothing more is heard of marriage, or of a son in whom the friend's beauty will be reproduced; but the theme of identity with a second self maintains its place as a major preoccupation of the sequence.

We now recognise the imaginative significance of the poet's repeated assertions that he and the friend share a single identity, that he is able to assume the personal attributes of the other, and that in loving the friend he loves himself. If the Sonnets describe Shakespeare's association with Herbert there will be no need to take such remarks seriously: they represent a mixture of wit, hyperbole and courtly compliment whose intentions alone are important, and which throws no light on the actual nature of the supposed liaison. But if the meaning of the Sonnets lies within the imaginative experience which they represent, these claims to shared identity are not to be mistaken for courtly extravagance. To the contrary, they form a vital centre of Shakespeare's creative attention. It is no valid objection that the poet of the Sonnets, whomever we take him to be, must recognise that he and his friend are in fact distinct individuals; for Shakespeare's imaginative purpose is to represent a form of experience which blurs such rational distinction and allows one to participate in the being and identity of the other. The poet is both himself and another; and the other who is not the poet is a second near-identical form of himself. The relationship of these selves, who are both separate and identical, is not susceptible of rational explanation; and by representing it in poetic terms Shakespeare does not invite us to suppose that it can be understood in some less paradoxical form. To offer a précis of the poet's remarks would be pointless. Their meaning cannot be separated from the terms in which it is expressed.

The need to respect this integrity of expression is made especially clear by Sonnet 62, which treats the poet's dualism as an almost explicit issue. An account of this poem in terms of story would explain that the poet is first presenting himself as though he had the friend's good looks and vanity,

> Methinks no face so gracious is as mine,
> No shape so true, no truth of such account;

and then being recalled by his mirror to the unwelcome facts of his worn and aged appearance. It would argue that the 'sin of self-love' to which the poet confesses is not simply vanity, but love of the friend whom he regards as himself, and that the face and figure which he describes as 'mine' are in fact those of the friend whose identity he shares. This explanation is confirmed in the couplet, where the poet clears up the confusion by telling his friend that he has been borrowing his personal attributes:

> 'Tis thee, myself, that for myself I praise;
> Painting my age with beauty of thy days.

Using the same term in two different senses does not entirely dispel the ambiguity of the poem; and although the line can be made to yield a plain sense–'It's you, my *alter ego*, whose attributes I speak of as my own'–an unequivocal statement was evidently not to Shakespeare's purpose. Some element of uncertainty remains, and ought not to be reduced in the interests of a clarity which the poet did not intend. At this point it becomes relevant to observe that whatever may be implied, the friend is nowhere explicitly addressed in this sonnet. For the purposes of the story, we may assume that 'thy days' are his, and that he is 'thee' in 1.13; but nothing in the poem itself shows that two distinct figures are involved. Rather the opposite is true; for the poet argues that the second person is himself. We may choose to regard this as a conceit, and to represent the meaning of the sonnet by a plain paraphrase which resolves the muddle of identities; making it clear that when the poet speaks of defining 'for myself mine own worth', he is speaking of the friend's qualities and not of his own. If so, we disregard Shakespeare's consistently developed purpose of clouding the issue which paraphrase would simplify and rationalise. We do better to assume that he intends the poem to say what it does. Its speaker is not a simple or a single being, but a figure containing a double identity, each part of which can be addressed, perhaps with a difference of intonation, as 'myself'. To assume that the poet regards the friend as a second self does not go far enough: in this sonnet the two identities are treated as interchangeable, to the extent that the admissions of the octet may be read as coming from either figure. The self-infatuated speaker who thinks 'no face so gracious is as mine' may be the poet who feels the friend's beauty to be his own; or the friend himself, in whose persona the poet is speaking. To himself, he is the friend; not in the sense of the convention which allows lovers to exchange identities, but in respect of the double personality of which he is part. His illusion persists until he is confronted by his reflection:

But when my glass shows me myself indeed,
Beated and chopped with tanned antiquity,
Mine own self-love quite contrary I read.

Inwardly he is one being, outwardly another; and what he calls 'myself' is both. Shakespeare has left the simple narrative basis of the Sonnets behind, and is extemporising upon the imaginative concepts developed from the relationship of poet and friend. He cannot be recalled from this point to the basic circumstances of the story, and this sonnet is not accountable in those plain narrative terms. To understand it, we must follow Shakespeare through the imaginative experience to which the poem provides a sensitive index.

Not every sonnet offers such an equivocal account of the curious partnership in which the poet is involved. In other poems the speaker comments more straightforwardly on his relationship with a friend who, whatever unusual traits he possesses, is evidently a distinct human being who can be absent on a journey, in the company of other friends, and addressed by a rival poet. This does not invalidate the fact that a number of sonnets refer to the friend as though he was neither entirely substantial nor independent of the poet: a circumstance duplicated in the poet's admitted inability to lead a happy existence when separated from the friend. A reading of the whole sequence is likely to leave an impression of the friend as a being who fluctuates between substance and shadow, now actual and now a figure of the poet's interior life. If we begin by assuming that the friend is Herbert, Southampton, or some other noble patron, such fluctuations of being will arouse no interest. At different times Shakespeare's mode of address is more or less particular; that is all. To speak as though the friend were a creation of his mind, or an aspect of the poet's personality not completely integrated with the rest, is a whimsical fancy which the reader can ignore or replace by some commonsense

equivalent. But poetry does not treat the world of common-sense; and some readers may suppose that the friend
remains unidentified not because Shakespeare has been discreet
but because he was neither describing nor trying to imagine a
fully definite person. If there had been some real need for dis-
cretion, it would have been better to have written no sonnets
about the friend. A reader who is prepared to accept the Sonnets
as a poem, and to search for a meaning compatible with
imaginative experience, will not wish to emend or paraphrase
the often paradoxical terms in which the friend is presented.
Shakespeare is to be taken at his word, or not at all.

The final impression left by the Sonnets is that the poet, who
may or may not represent Shakespeare in this respect, is not
certain whom he is addressing. The puzzled questioning which
opens Sonnet 53 seems to spring from the poet's sudden
recognition that the friend's teasingly cryptic nature makes him
a figure impossible to understand or define:

> What is your substance, whereof are you made,
> That millions of strange shadows on you tend?

Even those sonnets which address the friend as a normally
substantial being are not always certain of him. When his
nature is not equivocal, his sincerity is often in doubt; and the
poet suffers much from the friend's inconstancy, which develops
towards the hypocrisy and untruthfulness of being which are
later disclosed. There is a case for seeing the friend's duplicity
as an imaginatively parallel form of the indefiniteness which
the poet struggles to resolve in other sonnets. Whether he is
simply a charming hypocrite, 'Thy looks with me, thy heart
in other place', or a shadowy notional being from whom the
poet cannot entirely disengage himself, the friend is an essentially equivocal figure. At the simplest level of expression he
represents a contradiction between facial semblance and inward
nature which defies detection, for although

In many's looks the false heart's history
Is writ in moods and frowns and wrinkles strange,
[93

the friend's physical beauty is so absolute that no tell-tale mark
of his falsity can encroach upon it. At the further end of
Shakespeare's imaginative scale he is projected as something
hardly more definite than a state of existence, whose personal
identity is in doubt:

Who is it that says most, which can say more
Than this rich praise, that you alone are you?
[84

The compliment acts as cover to some typical questioning of
the friend's uncertain nature: the courtly poet who assures his
patron that he is the nonpareil is in league with the restless
enquiring spirit who asks whether the formula 'you alone are
you' sums up all that can be said of the friend's identity. His
remark is characteristically ambiguous. No one but the friend
can be 'you', though elsewhere the poet claims to have a share
in this other self, and describes the friend as 'all the better part
of me'. His claim helps us to recognise that 'you alone' does
not only mean 'no one but you'. The less obvious sense, 'you
by yourself', and by implication 'you without me', turns
attention back upon the dualistic relationship which holds the
poet and his mysterious friend together though never quite
uniting them. The fact which the poet frequently acknowledges, that he can have no separate existence apart from the
friend, could be equally relevant for his partner: each depends
upon the other for his being, in the way that a reflected image
depends upon the solid object which it mirrors; and cannot
exist independently. If this is so, 'you alone' has no being;
for in the relationship which the Sonnets describe each self is
partly integrated with the other, to the extent that 'myself'
has no certain application to either of them, but refers to both

at once. The poet may object that this relationship frustrates his wish to praise the friend;

> What can mine own praise to mine own self bring,
> And what is't but mine own when I praise thee?
>
> [39

and propose to break up this restricting partnership:

> Even for this, let us divided live,
> And our dear love lose name of single one;
> That by this separation I may give
> That due to thee which thou deserv'st alone.

The proposal is an unconvincing gesture towards a personal independence which would bring the poet not liberty of action but the distress of a severed personality. In the absence of the friend, or when he himself makes a journey, he admits the distraction of mind caused by temporary physical separation: 'debarred the benefit of rest',

> When day's oppression is not eased by night,
> But day by night and night by day oppressed.
>
> [28

He cannot break away from the friend. Even when his affection is answered by disloyalty and unkindness the poet makes no attempt to dissociate himself from the friend, and to dissolve their partnership: instead, he defects from his own cause and supports the friend's attempts to discredit him. Those who favour a literal interpretation of the Sonnets see his behaviour as a supreme expression of selfless love for an undeserving friend. A reading which takes Shakespeare's imaginative purposes into account will see the poet adopting the attitude of his second self in order to preserve the unanimity of their relationship. If there is a threat of rejection by the other, he counters it by denying all interest in his primary self, and shifting the focus of his being to the self which is attempting to repudiate him:

> Upon thy side against myself I'll fight,
> And prove thee virtuous, though thou art forsworn.
>
> [88

His action is contradictory, but not self-defeating. If this other being were simply Shakespeare's patron, the poet's eagerness to associate himself with the friend's disloyal impulse could be seen as an ignoble attempt to curry favour in a desperate situation; but imaginatively, as the Sonnets continue to insist, this second person is part of himself. Whoever is speaking in the Sonnets is obsessed by a need to integrate himself with an elusive second being who, despite his intimate kinship with the speaker, repeatedly attempts to break off their association. In terms of story, the poet's efforts to circumvent these moves may seem either self-abnegating or undignified, according to individual judgement; but these narrative circumstances are to be seen as the correlative of Shakespeare's imaginative concern, and not as its subject. The figures of the poet and his friend stand in a metaphorical relationship to the form of intensely inward experience or apprehension which Shakespeare is working out in writing the Sonnets. They indicate, but do not define or elucidate, the nature of whatever buried impulse struggles to realise itself through the figures and events of the sequence: an impulse which continues to manifest itself by moulding to its will part of the essential substance of the narrative poems and the plays.

The critic's task must be to offer some elucidation of the problems which he brings to light. To explain fully the inner significance of the Sonnets would become possible only if we had access to the working of Shakespeare's mind; for where historical interpretation of the Sonnets turns attention outwards, towards the society and environment in which the poet moved, an enquiry of the kind attempted in this book must end by trying to understand the imaginative purposes which impelled and directed Shakespeare's writing. Since we have no reason to suppose that Shakespeare himself consciously recognised or understood these purposes, the task of interpretation is doubly difficult; and the critic may find himself in the presumptuous position of claiming to understand the inner significance of the Sonnets more clearly than their author. This is a risk which he must accept; defending himself by arguing that the study of the mind in this century has brought about a new awareness of man's mental processes, and provided a means of interpreting impulses of thought whose existence had not previously been acknowledged or investigated. About the working of the creative imagination we still know very little; nothing more, in effect, than can be gathered inductively from the work of outstandingly gifted writers, who seem compelled occasionally to represent something of their creative experience in what they write. It remains to offer the suggestion that the dualism of the Sonnets, which extends to the narrative poems and runs through Shakespeare's dramatic work as an unwearied motif, represents a condition of his imaginative experience without which his creative activity could not have been carried on.

The Sonnets, the narrative poems and the early history-plays have the common theme of a self-destructive struggle within a body too deeply divided against itself to achieve unity of being. The different attempts of Venus, Tarquin and the poet of the Sonnets to make themselves one with another encounter the same check: the partner refuses to give himself, or herself, to the union proposed by the other; and instead of merging peacefully their contrary natures remain fiercely opposed. For Lucrece the conflict of natures induced by rape, which implants a hateful alien self within her, is too painful to be borne; and by killing herself she demonstrates the self-destructiveness of the unresolved conflict that is a major imaginative concern of Shakespeare's early work. The pronounced contrast between the figures of the abortive partnership might have helped to bring about a binding relationship, where likeness would repel; but these opposites are so extreme and mutually contradictory that they find no meeting-point. The harsh masculine ferocity of Tarquin is violently drawn towards the gentle modesty of Lucrece, but she is revolted by the hideousness of his revealed nature in the same way as his moral being is outraged by the fury of his physical appetite, and just as unable to adapt herself to its ugly intentions. Between the poet and his friend the differences are less extreme, and the one-sided desire for union does not include any such threat of savage violation for the unwilling partner; but in their quieter mode the Sonnets are occupied by the same frustrated urge towards integration. As a human figure, the friend is the poet's antitype: young, handsome and distinguished where the other is unrecognised and disfigured by age; fickle and calculating where the poet is unvaryingly constant and sincere. Despite their differences, the poet knows the friend to be a self with whom his own personality is involved, and longs to be integrated with this complementary being; but the differences present an insuperable barrier to the state of single identity which he pursues throughout the sequence.

Although repeatedly disappointed, the poet's desire for integration does not diminish: rather, it supplies the energy of his argument as he continues to explore his ambiguous relationship with the friend and to propose fresh means of sharing identity with him. Something similar seems to be true of Lucrece after the rape. From the quiescence of single being she is transformed into a self-contradictory figure who is both herself and Tarquin, and who is driven by the energies of conflict called out when an alien self invades her previously single identity. Under pressure of an intense desire to repudiate the hateful partner who now shares her identity, she becomes a dynamic figure seeking a form of self-expression that will both externalise her inner conflict and terminate the suffering which it causes. She finds what she is seeking in an act which represents the irreparable split which her personality has undergone; dividing herself against herself as though to distinguish the irreconcilable elements of the bifold being which she has acquired, and wielding the knife as Tarquin to destroy the innocent life of Lucrece. Her suicide is an acted metaphor of conflict within the self in terms immediately suggestive of art, and in particular of the means by which Shakespeare represents happenings within the private experience of his characters. It invites us to consider how far he may be representing in Lucrece the conditions under which his own creative energies are aroused and directed, and how in dissipating themselves by giving body to his imaginative experience they leave an imprint of the stimulus which called those energies into being.

The evident analogy between Lucrece's acted metaphor and the kind of poetic representation used by Shakespeare provides some initial reason for supposing that Lucrece stands in some close degree of relationship with her author. To the extent that she enacts highly subjective experience in terms of a physical equivalent, she can be seen as a modest counterpart of Shakespeare. Beyond this we can only surmise what further parallel exists; but in a field that encloses nothing more tangible than movements of creative consciousness, no more certain form of investigation is possible. When Lucrece acts-out the loathing which one of her selves feels towards the other, she also discloses the source of the energy which drives her to present her momentary play of the two persons she has become. This sudden release of creative potential reveals an ability which Lucrece has acquired in consequence of the profound disturbance of her personality: a force which stamps its own sharply divided image upon the scene she enacts. It seems likely that the source of Shakespeare's creative energy lay in some kindred form of conflict within the self, which both supplied the driving impulse of his work and left its own characteristic mark upon the writing which it impelled: likely because it might explain why dualistic figures and concepts are so habitually associated with the deeply imaginative movements of Shakespeare's consciousness. The contradictory being who is both Lucrece and Tarquin, and who executes justice upon one in the name of the other, does not share Shakespeare's obsession with dualism: she is a figure of that obsession. Not she but Shakespeare is the author of the play she dies performing. If anything can be gathered from her behaviour about the working of Shakespeare's imagination, the evidence is more direct than the seeming parallel suggests.

Simply expressed, the implications of Lucrece's experience are that the imaginative stimulus of Shakespeare's poetry came from some conflict within himself, whose tensions supplied the creative drive of his work; and that the dualistic figures which force themselves upon his imagination reflect the disturbance within Shakespeare's personality that is the starting-point of his creative activity. The suggestion that Shakespeare was himself a deeply divided figure does not imply mental illness, but contends that for him the creative process was inseparable from a sense of enmity and disquiet within the self. In the plays the scope and variety of dramatic action obscures Shakespeare's preoccupation with self-conflict; but in the severely limited field of the Sonnets, whose story rarely involves more than two figures, his imaginative concern with this subject becomes difficult to overlook. The poet's prolonged questioning of his relationship with the linked self with whom he cannot become integrated, yet from whom he cannot break away, isolates the element of dualism in Shakespeare's work and concentrates attention upon it. Where Lucrece wishes frantically to dissociate herself from the contaminating partnership forced upon her by Tarquin, the poet of the Sonnets pleads to be amalgamated with the shadow-being without whom he feels incomplete. An awareness of dualistic conflict within the self remains a dominant theme in both works, without respect to the form in which it is presented. The violent impulse of one character to be detached from a loathsome partner, and the impatient desire of another to be integrated with the complementary half of a twofold self, impel similar drives within the personality but lead to the same frustration. The divided self can neither be unified nor separated into its constituent selves. This condition of the poet's relationship with the friend of the Sonnets finally rebuts any simple assumption that these two figures can be identified with actual historical persons. If Shakespeare is represented in the Sonnets, he is not the poet alone but both figures, who are to be seen as positive and negative forms of the same self. The attempts to resolve the duplicity of the self's relationships with this counterpart are defeated; but in wrestling with his imaginative obsession Shakespeare gives body to the shifting impulses of his creative consciousness, and fulfils himself as a poet.

Index of Names

INDEX

Neilson, W. A., 16

Onions, C. T., 66 n.
Othello, 186

Passionate Pilgrim, The, 18
Prelude, The, 2

Raleigh, W., 5
Rape of Lucrece, The, 101 n., 173, 174, 176, 177–86, 187, 196, 197
Reed, E. B., 13
Resolution and Independence, 15
Richard III, 187, 188–9
Robertson, J. M., 13

Schlegel, A. W. von, 4
Schlegel, F. von, 4
Southampton, Earl of, 203
Spenser, E., 3
Stirling, B., 93 n.

Symonds, J. A., 10

Tempest, The, 187
Thorndike, A. H., 16
Tieck, L., 4
Tucker, T. G., 11, 12, 85
Twelfth Night, 123, 147, 160
Two Gentlemen of Verona, 191–6

Verity, A. W., 5
Venus and Adonis, 132 n., 136, 145, 151, 173, 174, 175, 176, 177

W. H., Mr, 13, 18
Westminster Review, The, 12
Wilson, J. D., 7, 17, 43, 46, 67, 77, 138, 139, 166
Wordsworth, W., 1, 2, 4, 5, 9, 10, 13, 15

Young, M. McC., 13

Index of Sonnets individually referred to

INDEX